Judy— This doesn't have the majesty of "I Ching", but you might find it of some interest.— Please accept it with my "thank you"!

— Sincerely,

Marie W.

2-10-76

Teaching and Philosophy: A Synthesis

HOUGHTON MIFFLIN COMPANY · BOSTON
New York   Atlanta   Geneva, Illinois   Dallas   Palo Alto

MARIE E. WIRSING
University of Colorado Denver Center

Teaching and Philosophy: A Synthesis

Printed in the U.S.A.

Library of Congress Catalog Card Number: 70–162055

ISBN: 0-395-12537-5

Education is one of those subjects which oscillates wildly from practice to theory and back again. When lay Americans discuss what should be going on in the schools, gearing up for the defeat of the next bond issue, they prefer to elaborate their argument at the level of what is happening to their Johnnies on a given Tuesday morning. But when the editorial writers and academic pamphleteers get going, their rhetoric talks grandly of the American character and of the place education should occupy in that vague thesaurus of values now known as "national priorities."

Professors in our colleges of education also swing between these polarities. There are those who go into the classrooms of the nation every day to supervise and instruct the student-teacher in training, convinced that the improvement of education occurs right where they are, in physical proximity to real boys and girls. Back on campus, there are those who have pondered the more abstruse features of learning theory, curriculum design, and the epistemology of educational policy-making, and believe that reform must be worked out at their desks and in their seminar rooms with a theoretical redefinition of public learning itself. As every professor of education knows, the tension between these two groups is universal, constant, and frequently angry.

In this volume, Professor Wirsing shows a way of embracing these polarities, of building lines of communication and understanding between the conceptualizer and the situationist. With a careful logic, she reveals the flaw in the old, transmit-the-culture theory of schooling. She then approaches the "nuts and bolts" aspect of the *act* of teaching by way of a philosophical examination of the *purposes* of teaching. When she emerges at the other side of the argument, she puts forward what she calls a working "common denominator" of what moves and animates all good education.

The author speaks from an unusual response to her own experience in the teaching business. In her time, she has "done her own thing," both as a teacher and as a teacher of teachers. But she realizes better than most that the idiosyncratic approach to teaching can carry one just so far; a teaching "presence" is not all there is to the practice of education. Sooner or later, the individual's style must be fitted into the larger frame of the institution, augmented by the other styles—both of the teachers and of the students—which co-exist and operate there. It is the nimble orchestration of these many personalized modes of teaching and learning which makes possible the vibrant and exciting Tuesday mornings which the nation's parents are asking for.

Preparing teachers for such schools is a difficult art. Those professors of education who are serious about carrying their theories into the schools will find Professor Wirsing someone they can listen to and identify with. But, more important, their students—those in training approaching or engaged in student teaching—will find it easy to respond to this author. Here is a pro who has been there and come back to tell about it.

Van Cleve Morris

ACKNOWLEDGEMENTS

When a writer attempts to acknowledge those who have been responsible for the general development of his thinking, he faces a monumental task. Like most, I prefer to credit myself with some originality and at least the occasional contribution of a fresh idea. However, the truth is I find that I owe a heavy debt to the countless others who have had an impact on my life. Although any errors of judgment reflected in this volume must be claimed exclusively as my own, I would like to acknowledge with sincere gratitude those many persons who have played a major role in my on-going education. In particular, I wish to express deep thanks to:

My students at the University of Colorado Denver Center, who provoked most of the thoughts I have tried to come to grips with herein, and who remain the chief catalysts in the reconstruction of my own ideas.

The numerous friends and colleagues who read and criticized this manuscript during its preparatory stages, and who gave me innumerable suggestions for improving it.

Professor Francis Brush of the Department of Philosophy at the University of Denver, who during the years of my graduate studies gave me a perspective on educational foundations that clarified and deepened my own position at the same time that it opened the way to understanding, appreciating, and learning from positions different from my own.

Professor Philip Perdew of the School of Education at the University of Denver, who taught me a profound lesson: that the support for one point of view need not depend upon the destruction of another point of view. It will please me very much if he finds this lesson reflected throughout the body of what follows.

Professor Van Cleve Morris, Dean of the College of Education, University of Illinois at Chicago Circle, who was kind enough to review the entire manuscript. His critical eye and penetrating judgment helped me to vastly improve the organization of this volume. My debt to Professor Morris is considerable.

Professor Louis Fischer of the School of Education at the University of Massachusetts, who also read the complete manuscript and offered a number of valuable suggestions.

John, Loretta, Robert, and Nancy Wirsing, who were a major sustaining force through their affection, advice, encouragement, and patience. Their scholarship and interest served as a continuing sounding board during the compilation of this work.

Edna F. Denniston, teacher and respected friend, who in her eightieth year could write to me: "One of the best things about living is the discovery that there is always something *un*discovered to search for and enjoy."

My mother, Marie Alice Wirsing, who read and criticized these pages many times while they were in the making and to whom this volume is affectionately dedicated.

M.E.W.

CONTENTS

THE TWAIN
SHALL MEET

At least three good friends are likely to shake their heads in dismay when this small volume appears in print. They were with me a few years ago in Guadalajara, Mexico, when— freely opinionating after a relaxing vacation—I vowed that I would never get caught in the publishing game that divides the energies of so many college professors. "I really like to teach," I expounded, "and that's a full-time job in every sense of the term. Furthermore, it's hard to find a book in education that hasn't been said before. If anything exciting is going to happen in the preparation of teachers, I think it is more likely to occur from a dynamic interchange between flesh-and-blood students and teachers in higher education than from the exposure of novice teachers to the written admonitions of Solomon himself!"

Looking back on Guadalajara from the vantage point of today, I must admit that I am still in agreement with my earlier declarations. I still think that those of us who teach in colleges and universities need to regard our teaching responsibilities as the full measure of our professional lives. I still think that what happens between people—not what happens between a student and a book—has the greater impact in the education of new teachers. And I still think that enormous quantities of ideas about education already have appeared in print and could well be tangled with prior to one's adding more of the same to library shelves. Nonetheless, this volume grew out of other convictions that were not so apparent to me in Guadalajara, and the book's purpose, I hope, will evidence sufficient good faith to vindicate my efforts in the eyes of my three friends.

The experiences I have had during my teaching assignments at the University of Colorado Denver Center have largely shaped this book. Working with pre-service students in secondary methodology courses and with in-service teachers in philosophy of education courses, I have become increasingly aware that for many classroom teachers these two areas—methodology and philosophy—represent the twain which never meet. In methods classes, I have noted the puzzlement of students when I encourage them to relate their ideas about classroom practice to their foundational ideas. By the same token, I have observed how easily experienced teachers get carried away in philosophic discourse, failing to relate those ideas to what they are doing in their own classrooms with their own students.

This book, therefore, makes its appearance to present my plea for a wholistic approach to classroom teaching. I will attempt to demonstrate that philosophy and methods are not two separate operations but denote one process looked at from opposite ends. And I will take the position that a working understanding of the full process is essential to anyone who would be an educator and not a mere technician.

I had a particular reader in mind as I wrote this book—the person standing at the threshold of his teaching career. My comments have been directed to him because, quite frankly, I see him as the pivotal figure in America's educational future. Unlike many of his predecessors, he reflects the agonizing questioning and probing of values and behavior which are symptomatic of an increasingly sensitive and intelligent generation. I have endeavored to meet the level of intellectual maturity warranted by this contemporary student. But in the spirit of today's youth, I have not drawn fixed parameters around my message—that is, it is not my intention that this work be restricted to novice teachers or to "courses" in education. If the book is substantive, perhaps it will encourage needed dialogue among educators in general, wherever they may be functioning in the American educational system and however experienced they may be.

I have focused my attention on the secondary school and selected my illustrations from that level because this has been the setting for the development of my own professional concerns during the past ten years. However, I am very mindful that the usefulness of the ideas I have dealt with is not confined to the high school classroom. To believe that a book of this sort has implications for only one level of the total American educational system would be shortsighted—much like the case of a physician who examines only his patient's heart and ignores the condition of the rest of the body. Philosophic considerations are not germane merely because of the age of one's students. The shared experiences of my graduate students, fully half of whom come from elementary-school teaching backgrounds, have convinced me further of an underlying commonality in our educational concerns and problems. In this recognition I invite the beginning elementary teacher to explore these ideas along with his colleagues in the junior and senior high schools; I explicitly encourage him to transpose my secondary illustrations to his own school setting.

The key notion which I have examined is that a teacher's methodology reflects his basic assumptions. Consciously or unconsciously, every teacher makes myriad decisions each day in terms of his particular stock of underlying beliefs. The way in which he ascertains his objectives and then selects, structures, and teaches his content depends upon the theoretical framework in which he operates—what he believes about the good life, how people learn, and what they need to learn. In view of the responsibilities of the teaching role, these decisions which the teacher makes can have a far-reaching impact on the lives of all concerned. When the teacher approaches such decisions blindly, the relationship between methods and philosophy can and often does reflect a discontinuity of thought. Hence when such a teacher is pushed to the wall for a justification of his teaching behavior, he finds himself in the disturbing situation of operating without a rationale that makes sense to anyone, including himself. Therefore, a conscious linkage between philosophical belief and teaching practice needs to be sought from the outset of one's professional preparation.

Although I would argue that age and experience do not preclude a rigorous self-examination, reorganization, and integration of one's thinking patterns, I also hold that if the relationship between theory and methods is not perceived in the initial stages of professional preparation, the relationship is not so likely to be appreciated after the teaching license has been obtained. One might make an analogy to the law student who busies himself for years in learning the techniques of courtroom debate and all the intricacies of constructing legal documents. The chances are high that a law student with such a perspective will continue to focus his attention on the technical aspects of his work once he passes his bar examination and hangs out his shingle. It is unlikely that he will achieve the vision and stature of a Marshall, Holmes, or Brandeis during his legal career. What distinguished the careers of these men was their wholistic approach to their profession—their constant efforts to relate technical considerations to underlying foundational questions.

This wholistic approach to the professional life was illustrated a few years ago by Earl Warren when a lawyer was energetically arguing a case before the Supreme Court on the basis of technicalities. At one point in the presentation, Chief' Justice Warren is reported to have leaned over the bench and queried, "But is it fair?" Whatever the merits of the particular case, Warren's question revealed a bent of mind and an outlook which went far beyond a superficial concern for courtroom debate and the construction of legal documents. In a similar sense the case for relating the technical considerations of teaching to underlying foundational questions will be made throughout this book.

I do not mean to imply that teaching methods are or should be linked automatically to particular theories. Almost any single method can be used by teachers with entirely different reasons for using it. For example, the discussion method is used at some time by almost every teacher; however, the reason for using it, the assessment of its effectiveness in a particular class, and the evaluation of student responses will depend upon the basic outlook of the teacher involved.

If I succeed in making but a single point with the reader, let that point be the fact that two teachers can *do* exactly the same thing in a classroom for entirely different reasons, and the *covert reasons* are as important as the *overt actions*. It is as crucial to communicate this relationship to prospective teachers as the technical know-how of methodology, and this relationship was the criterion for choosing the materials included in this work. The idea is developed more fully in Part One, the background against which the subsequent parts have been written.

The reader should be forewarned that if he looks for detailed treatment of teaching techniques herein, he will be disappointed in the sparsity of his findings. This volume is not offered to replace the dozens of methodology books already available to the classroom practitioner. Many of these other works are far more comprehensive in scope and give much greater attention to such specifics as phrasing questions for class discussions, designing unit and lesson plans, organizing role-playing sessions, utilizing simulation games, preparing students for oral reports, grouping, developing testing materials, and scores of other classroom activities. Instead of attempting to write exhaustively about as many of these teaching techniques as possible, I have deliberately been selective and included classroom procedures *only when they illustrate significant theoretical concerns.*

Nor is this volume intended to serve as a philosophy primer for the classroom teacher. That purpose can be met by any number of published scholarly works in educational philosophy. Instead, I have attempted to develop a way of looking at the entire phenomenon of teaching. It is my belief that persons who are initiating their professional careers first need to be helped to see the necessary continuity between both ends of the teaching process. Then, as they focus their attention on particular techniques in their specialized methods courses and experiment with those techniques in their student-teaching situations, their selection and development of techniques can be accomplished against an intellectual framework that has a recognized point of origin and clearly perceived end goals.

The reader also should be forewarned that neutrality has not played a role in the writing of this book. Elsewhere I have discussed the folly of it. I admit to having a definite perspective, and whereas I have considered alternative viewpoints throughout this work, I have not attempted to conceal my own preferences. When such preferences are not obvious in the treatment of the content, I have made an effort to set forth my position. Also, I have made liberal use of my own experiences to illustrate various ideas. This I have done not with the aim of presenting a self-righteous success formula of my own, but in the belief that teaching must be approached from an individual orientation. What emerges in the following pages, therefore, might be described as the intensely personal outlook of one educator. The desire to share this outlook arises primarily from my conviction that teachers should be encouraged to work their way through a wide assortment of ideas during the course of their professional preparation. And although an impersonal exposition of ideas might afford me the comfort of considerably less opposition, the deliberate thrust of a particular point of view can have the educational advantage of provoking far greater critical response. Consequently, in tangling with the ideas that follow, the reader is invited to separate *for himself* the wheat from the chaff.

Part One
Where Do You Begin?

CHAPTER ONE

THE CLIMATE OF
CHANGE

"How can I change my son's classroom situation?" The question was directed to me by one of my graduate students in education—a secondary teacher by training and experience, and a warm, sensitive, and perceptive young woman. She was deeply concerned about the learning atmosphere in the kindergarten class where her little boy was being exposed to American public education for the first time. According to her, the teacher regarded herself as an unquestioned authority on all matters, a giver of knowledge, and a stern disciplinarian. Heightening the anxiety of the mother over her son's welfare in this conformity-inducing climate was her growing awareness that the boy seemed to genuinely enjoy school in general and his kindergarten teacher in particular. "This teacher has tenure," she went on to explain, "and she probably will influence children's thinking for the next twenty years if someone doesn't do something about her!"

After discussing the situation with her at some length and

sharing my own discomfort in the face of such teaching, I felt it necessary to answer the initial question with some questions of my own. I asked if she wasn't seeking advice on how to make over the kindergarten teacher in her own image of what a good teacher should be, and on how to make over the classroom in her own image of a good curriculum. If this was the case, I further queried, what then was she projecting for all American education and for all teachers? In short, I questioned the implications of the very question she had posed.

After some serious reflection, the troubled mother conceded that she indeed had been unconsciously looking for precisely such advice. As we talked further, she decided that she could provide many other kinds of significant learning experiences for her son—and could do this without undermining the kindergarten teacher or her son's fondness for that teacher. For example, she saw that since her son was in the habit of relating what he had learned from his teacher each day, a relatively easy way of broadening his horizons would be for her to adopt the attitude "That's very interesting! Let me show you still other ways of looking at the same thing. . . ."

THE FOCUS ON DOING

As illustrated in the above conference, there is a marked tendency for both teachers and their critics to focus attention on the "doing" aspects of education. The young woman was eager to "do" something about another teacher whose visible teaching performance did not suit her. In a similar sense, the visible act of teaching history, English, science, mathematics, foreign languages, and other subjects weighs far more heavily in the concerns of most classroom teachers than the theoretical *whys* which underlie their activities.

One needs only to attend a few local, regional, or national education conferences to gain a feel for the "doing" preferences of teachers. The perennial search among convention-goers is for stimulating speakers who outline clear-cut directions for improving classroom teaching and who expound on definite techniques for implementing such directions. The speaker who does not devote sufficient attention to how-to-do-it invariably leaves a confused and dissatisfied audience.

Symptomatic of the preoccupation with the visible dimension of teaching is the attitude toward methodology courses. In teacher-education programs, methodology is regarded as the nuts-and-bolts aspect of teaching; it is what you actually do in a classroom with live students who have been entrusted to your instruction. Usually education students enroll in such courses to learn the specifics of the best way to teach. If the methods course is geared to high-powered, how-to-do-it instruction, the chances are good that many of them will regard it as the only practical education course.

However, the prospective teacher who thinks that his methods courses will equip him with a ready-made set of answers to questions of what to do and how to do it is destined for disillusionment. Unless he insulates himself early in his career behind a thick coating of apathy (and some do), eventually he will be forced into the painful recognition that *very different sets of answers exist for every conceivable question about classroom teaching.* This fact will become apparent as soon as he attempts to genuinely communicate with other teachers and with administrators, students, parents, and school board members.

Therefore, if the prospective educator is to approach teaching with the conviction and inner strength born of a sense of direction that he himself has intelligently arrived at, he will begin his preparation by probing the foundations for doing. He will realize that methodology does not develop in a vacuum and that it does not represent a grab bag of tricks applicable for all teachers in all times and in all places. When he subsequently formulates his own teaching style and methodology, it will be as a conscious extension of the basic assumptions he holds about the good, the true, and the beautiful—the basic assumptions against which he determines *what is* and *what ought to be* in all human affairs, including education.

All that follows in this volume is an effort to demonstrate that a philosophical foundation is essential to the development of the professional, articulate educator.

THE VOICES OF EDUCATIONAL REFORM

It is difficult to imagine a time in American life when the *what is* and the *what ought to be* of our educational system have been under closer public scrutiny. Even the casual observer cannot miss the outpouring of articles arguing that our schools are not meeting the needs of our children, as well as the stream of critical letters to newspaper editors on the state of American education. As these words are being written, newspapers across the nation are filled with stories about student unrest. The mood which nurtured activism and open revolt among college students during the 1960's has seeped down to the high schools, and as we enter the new decade, turbulence there appears to forecast "the way it's going to be."[1] Beneath this turbulence one finds that high school students themselves are now voicing their dissatisfaction with the way in which they are being educated. And although many adults are reluctant to consider the legitimacy of such adolescent protest, it is often difficult to differentiate the battle cry of many students from that of prestigious educational spokesmen—for example, the first Secretary of Health, Education, and Welfare in the Nixon administration. In January, 1969, Robert Finch approached his new office by issuing a call for a dramatic shake-up to improve teaching throughout the entire educational system, from the kindergarten through the collegiate level.[2] Therefore, to say that we live in an era that strongly desires change is an understatement. In view of the present obvious turmoil, it is not unlikely that many persons considering a teaching career are themselves caught up in a crusading spirit for redirecting the course of American education.

The climate of change in our own times is reminiscent of the zealous crusading spirit which has dominated the thinking

[1] Diane Divoky, "Revolt in the High Schools," p. 83. See also "Collision Course in the High Schools," pp. 22–39; Theodore Roszak, *The Making of a Counter Culture*, pp. 1–82; and Charles A. Reich, *The Greening of America*, pp. 3–20.

[2] James Bow, "School Shake-up Could Help: Finch," p. 10. Cf. President Nixon's own subsequent call for "genuine reform" of elementary and secondary education in America: "Nixon Proposes School Reform," p. 1.

of other people and other times. During one stage of the French Revolution, for example, ardent reformers succeeded in removing traditional objects of worship from church altars; in place of what had been swept away they enshrined statues of the Goddess of Reason. The new religion flourished vigorously, if briefly, and all those who stood in its way were sacrificed in the name of progress.[3] It may be that we are witnessing a modern-day variation of this phenomenon. But instead of venerating the vacuous Goddess of Reason of the Jacobins, we have substituted our own vacuous Goddess of Change. However, in order that the reader does not summarily sweep me away as a champion of reactionary thinking in our own day, let me address myself to the very real need for change.

Without doubt, the growing awareness on the part of political figures, the general public, students, and educators that "something is wrong" with our schools and the drive to do something about the situation are potentially healthy, positive forces. Unfortunately, however, many of the resulting demands for educational change—like demands for other institutional change—are plagued by two states of mind that are neither healthy nor constructive: *narcissism* and *nonreflectiveness*. These states of mind, it should be noted, are not unique to our own era, to our own generation of reformers. Let us examine each in turn.

NARCISSISM

Narcissus, as the reader will recall, was the lad in classical mythology who fell in love with his own image reflected in a pool. In essence, a narcissistic attitude promotes the almost unconscious desire *to facilitate change in one's own direction*. The individual so afflicted wants all others to reflect what he himself holds to be good and desirable. Having others around him thinking and doing whatever he is thinking and doing undoubtedly supports him in his conviction that he is *right*.

[3] Leo Gershoy, *The French Revolution and Napoleon*, pp. 286–88.

Needless to say, to be convinced that one is right in one's pursuits is an emotionally comfortable and secure way of living—and of educating. However, a serious problem comes into focus with the recognition that history is filled with instances of genuinely dedicated people who have sought to remake the world (or aspects of the world) in their own image —with the unhappy chronicle of one disastrous confrontation after another.

Narcissism can be found in the present attacks by pressure groups on the textbooks used in our public schools. Although professional judgment might seem to be the logical determinant in the matter of selecting curriculum materials, in actuality classroom teachers often have little to say about the books they can make available to their students. Self-styled exponents of "Americanism," for example, have periodically attempted to purge the schools of textbooks which in their opinion contain undesirable and harmful ideas. One of the most powerful efforts was triggered by the 1959 *Textbook Study* sponsored by the Daughters of the American Revolution. This study analyzed 214 textbooks used in elementary and secondary schools throughout the nation. Only fifty of these met "minimum DAR standards"; the remaining texts all were branded "un-American." The major objection to many of the rejected textbooks was that they recommended supplementary readings by such distinguished authors as Ruth Benedict, Theodore H. White, Matthew Josephson, Langston Hughes, Margaret Mead, Gordon Allport, John King Fairbank, Lincoln Steffens, Richard Wright, and Bill Mauldin. This DAR report, which received the strong support of other like-minded pressure groups, motivated several state legislative bodies to investigate textbook selection procedures and in some instances to place control of such decisions in the hands of politically appointed state committees.[4]

There can be, of course, little quarrel with the right of pressure groups within American society to try to influence the nation's youth. However, it should be apparent that narcissism promotes activities that go far beyond the exercise of

[4] Jack Nelson and Gene Roberts, Jr., *The Censors and the Schools*, pp. 78–97.

grass-roots democracy. Such activities try to squeeze out all points of view which do not fit into the thought patterns of the special interest group. Success in these ventures is achieved largely through the creation of a social climate wherein the security of teachers is jeopardized unless they conform to the desired views.

Teacher security also can be threatened by narcissistic forces other than special-interest groups, which usually desire to control only particular aspects of education. A more subtle and insidious form of narcissism is that posed by some of our new technological and engineering skills and the blind, band-wagon espousal of these skills by our social Establishment. This new brand of narcissism goes far beyond the scope of special-interest groups in that it seeks to shape the *totality* of American education. Its impact is being felt, for example, by an experienced foreign language teacher in a high school. This man is very unhappy over the curriculum content of his courses. "I have to use programmed materials," he told me recently, "whether I want to or not!"

From the beginning of our national existence, the Establishment of American society, like that in all other societies, has attempted to make the public schools instruments of standardization and stabilization. In a very real sense, the Establishment historically has functioned as the largest of our country's pressure groups.[5] As long as other voices within our society have been able to promote the use of our public schools as centers of various kinds of innovation, differentia-tion, and change, the standardization and stabilization sought by the Establishments of the past never have been particularly successful. However, the Establishment of the present era has at its disposal the means to effect a massive, overwhelming

[5] In fairness to the reader I should clarify my own use of this much abused phrase "the Establishment." Although I do not regard the Estab-lishment as a centralized and readily identifiable unit of social power, I recognize that certain parallel ideas, attitudes, values, and practices dominate our institutional life. Persons and groups who reflect the dominant ideas and values of a given era do tend to command the policy-making machinery of the social institutions, including public education. Collectively such persons present a formidable united front, a front which I identify as the Establishment.

consolidation of the content and conduct of education in America. There is no question that agencies of technology and industry are compelling a reorientation of teaching and learning that dwarfs anything the DAR might have dreamed about in its wildest moments. It is apparent, too, that this reorientation is being promoted and funded in the awesome name of science, and that the intent of its promoters is to design *the way* of educating all persons to fit into the rapidly changing world of the twentieth century. James Ridgeway discussed the ramifications of the mounting technocracy as it appeared to him in June, 1966—a time which now is recognized as the infancy of a big new educational industry:

The leaders are well enough known: IBM and its subsidiary, Science Research Associates; RCA and Random House; the joint ventures of General Electric and Time, Inc.; Raytheon and D. C. Heath; General Telephone & Electronics, and *Reader's Digest*; Litton Industries; and the nest of education firms acquired by Xerox. . . . The philosophy that governs [the new industry's] overall development comes from the systems analysts around Secretary McNamara, who have worked hard to persuade both industry and the rest of the Administration that the systems approach is the best way to tackle the problems of the Great Society. Consequently the education businessmen don't look at their job from the standpoint of just selling one product, but rather with an eye to designing and carrying through several functions; that is, they want to design a school system, provide it with innovative materials and equipment, train the teachers how to use the equipment, and then test the finished product—in this case, the student as he comes out of one system and goes into another. The long-range thrust is toward making the computer into an effective teaching machine. If this can be done, the present school structure will radically change. It is conceivable that the school as we now know it will go out of existence altogether.[6]

[6] James Ridgeway, "Computer-Tutor," *The New Republic* (June 4, 1966), p. 19. Reprinted by permission of *The New Republic*, © 1966, Harrison-Blaine of New Jersey, Inc. See also Roszak, *Counter Culture*, pp. 5–22; Sue M. Brett, "The Federal View of Behavioral Objectives," in *On Writing Behavioral Objectives for English*, ed. John Maxwell and Anthony Tovatt, pp. 43–47; James Cass, "Profit and Loss in Education," pp. 39–40, and "Free Enterprise for Schools," pp. 58–59.

The systems approach to education has developed an impressive thrust indeed in the few years since Ridgeway's prediction. In view of the fact that the approach regards students as finished products—or in the jargon of the systems analysts as "inputs" and "outputs"—the implications for standardization and stabilization of the human material with which the schools work are staggering. In my opinion, the programmed mentalities of growing numbers of engineers, technicians, and researchers of human behavior make the narcissistic flag-waving of the DAR insignificant by comparison.

But educational narcissism is a mental outlook that is not restricted either to small special-interest groups or to the large Establishment agencies operating outside the schools. Teachers themselves frequently squeeze out student points of view that are not in harmony with their own. Success in these efforts is achieved through the creation of a classroom climate wherein the security of students is jeopardized unless they conform to the desired views. Security, in such instances, tends to be overtly or covertly tied to the ever-present specter of grades. In a microcosmic sense, some teachers actually project their own Establishmentlike front in their relationship with students. This relationship is as narcissistic and intimidating as anything conveyed by the larger social Establishment.

Not long ago, I observed a teacher-led discussion in a social studies class in a suburban junior high school. The Anglo teacher in charge of a class of all-Anglo students was attempting to get at some of the problems involved in the matter of busing Negro students from the inner-city to suburban schools. Although that teacher undoubtedly was conducting the class under the assumption that it was an open discussion in which all his students were free to express their opinions, his pivotal questions and his responses to student comments nonetheless led the students toward acceptance of his own convictions. Variations of "How would busing interfere with the right of people to live in neighborhoods and go to schools of their own choosing?" dominated this discussion, and every student response was examined against this question. What-

ever other rights might have been at stake here were minimized or ignored by the teacher. In a metropolitan area that
literally was seething with controversy over the cross-busing
issue, it was a curious spectacle to observe a class of thirty
students arrive at the unanimous conclusion that busing is
undesirable.

NONREFLECTIVENESS

The second unfortunate state of mind which colors our social
climate is that of nonreflectiveness, or superficial thinking.
When manifested in demands for educational change, such an
attitude implies *a reluctance on the part of the individual
seeking change to consider the full implications of what he
wants.* For example, countless educators express extreme dissatisfaction with the long-standing practice of training students to put little black marks in proper places on paper so
that students can be scored "objectively." Many educators
candidly admit that this practice of reducing the complex
phenomenon of learning to a collection of digital scores and
finally to an all-encompassing letter grade cannot be defended
intelligently. And many of those educators express unhap-
piness over the destructive impact of their grading practices
on their relationships with students. Yet those same critics
seldom work through the full implications of the changes they
seek in the evaluation process; the procedures they propose in
lieu of little black marks usually are vague. A vacuum is
thereby created in the matter of what and how to evaluate—a
vacuum not unlike those instances reported in Erich Fromm's
Escape from Freedom, in which men in their quest for freedom
repeatedly tore down existing systems only to discover that
they did not know what to do with their new-found freedom.
According to Fromm, those same persons ultimately responded by rejecting freedom and by replacing what they had
destroyed with more of the same under different names. In
brief, nonreflective thinking tends to generate circular behavior—as expressed in the classic French proverb, "The more
things change the more they remain the same."

Thus, despite the agonizing of many teachers over grading,
their failure to develop clear purpose and alternative procedures has sanctioned the great boom in standardized testing as

a means of improving education.[7] In 1962, the National Education Association's Joint Committee on Testing published a highly critical report on the nature, scope, and effects of testing in the secondary schools across the nation. The report emphasized the widespread misconceptions held by the general public as well as by many educators regarding the infallibility of standardized tests:

Standardized tests are mass-produced devices for rating individuals on certain limited and definable tasks that can be performed on a sheet of paper. The tasks, having been standardized on the basis of a wide range of population characteristics, must necessarily be pertinent for many. However, students perform differently at different times and under different circumstances, and no standardized instrument can *measure* traits not susceptible to quantification. This, of course, means that much important territory is overlooked. It has been demonstrated repeatedly that even when the greatest care has been exercised in constructing test items, there may be more than one *right* answer to some questions. These alternative answers are usually given by intelligent students who are temperamentally unable to confine themselves to a single *right* answer—not necessarily the *only* answer and sometimes not even the *best* answer. *Objectivity* in such cases pertains to the marking process; the questions asked are not objective.[8]

Unfortunately, the impressive cautions expounded in the NEA study have largely gone unheeded, for the use of standardized tests in the schools has vastly increased—to the current plans for a standardized national assessment of education.[9] But recognizing the prevalence of nonreflective thinking

[7] Standardized tests are instruments designed to measure segments of a certain area of knowledge and/or skills at a particular time. They are impersonal in that they are constructed by groups, agencies, or organizations outside a given classroom and usually by persons outside the local school district.

[8] Joint Committee on Testing: American Association of School Administrators, Council of Chief State School Officers, National Association of Secondary School Principals, *Testing, Testing, Testing* (Washington: National Education Association, 1962), pp. 16–17.

[9] Committee on Assessing the Progress of Education, *How Much Are Students Learning? Plans for a National Assessment of Education.*

among teachers, one can only conclude that any concrete means of handling the evaluation problem seems better than no means whatsoever. In the process, teachers relinquish to external authorities the responsibility for appraising pupil progress, and students continue to make foolish little black marks.

If education represented a fairly well-defined body of knowledge and practices, the above problems (and many others) resulting from narcissism and nonreflectiveness undoubtedly would lend themselves to easier resolution and mutual agreement among educators. By way of comparison, these particular attitudes do not pose difficulties of the same magnitude in the medical profession, in which the physical realm of concerns is of a much more cumulative nature. To be sure, physicians are not in accord on many matters. Nonetheless, one would expect to find widespread agreement among them that the techniques of today's heart surgeon are a significant improvement over the barber-surgeon of the medieval era. With each new medical breakthrough, comparatively little difficulty is encountered in effecting change in that direction among medical practitioners. A dramatic illustration is the Salk vaccine. After its introduction a few years ago, there was a rapid movement among the vast majority of physicians to immunize their patients against crippling polio. The results of the polio vaccine have been demonstrably positive, and few persons would seriously question that this medical innovation has been desirable.

But what needs to be recognized is the fact that the study and practice of education doesn't begin to lend itself to the demonstrability of the Salk vaccine. Because of its broad, complex nature and because its concerns go beyond physical well-being, education must deal with many ideas that are of a noncumulative nature.[10] For example, it would be impossible to demonstrate in a universally convincing way that Plato's

[10] For a discussion of the nature of noncumulative knowledge, see Robert K. Merton, *Social Theory and Social Structure*, pp. 27–30.

educational ideas are really not as good as those A. S. Neill expresses in *Summerhill,* or that desirable change really would occur if all classroom practitioners utilized programmed instruction or group encounter. Compared to medical innovators, educational innovators who desire to promote widespread change in a specific direction must do so against an infinitely more controversial backdrop.

The inherently noncumulative quality of education has had enormous implications for the shaping of the foundations of American public education. Our educational system, formed in a democratic atmosphere of many competing ideas, appears to have been built more upon an intellectual quagmire than upon a firm, well-ordered body of ideas. This situation is readily apparent to the teacher who struggles with the critical questions, Where do I begin? What do I change?

Nowhere are the foundational difficulties of our educational system more apparent than in the area of goals and values— that is, in the matter of *ultimate purposes* of education. Since teaching methodology is simply the means of seeking to achieve ultimate purposes, considerable attention needs to be given to this issue of goals and values. In the process, the entire foundational quagmire must be examined.

CHAPTER TWO

TRANSMITTING THE CORE VALUES: A DILEMMA

The traditional role of the teacher in our society, as in others, has been to pass on the culture. This has been regarded as a primary professional responsibility, and few educators have questioned the legitimacy or feasibility of it. But the assignment *should* be questioned seriously, if for no other reason than the existence of another revered tradition: *cultural pluralism.*

Our pluralism is the product of our unique history. No other nation on earth has been formed by the interaction of so many disparate cultures. And although different reasons prompted migrations to this country, it can be said that all these individuals and groups were responding in their own distinctive ways to the promise of "life, liberty, and the pursuit of happiness." This promise has become a cherished cornerstone of the American way of life, and individuals and groups are still responding to it *in their own distinctive ways.*

Simply stated, cultural pluralism implies the existence of

diverse basic values or assumptions[1] about what constitutes the good life. Consequently, if the educator in our public schools seeks to fulfill his declared role of transmitting the core values and to derive his methodology from such an overriding purpose, he will confront a dilemma of no small proportions in the contradictions that exist in the collective core values. To appreciate the complexity of this task, one needs only to sample the ideological core of American life as a whole—the heart of our principles and beliefs.

INDIVIDUALISM AND CONFORMITY

Americans, for example, have enshrined a belief in individualism. This doctrine is manifested in a thousand strands throughout our institutional life and our behavior patterns. It was immortalized in Emerson's "Whoso would be a man, must be a nonconformist." In education this particular belief is expressed in such efforts as "individualizing instruction" and in "meeting the needs of individual students." But Americans are also described as organization men seeking security at the price of individualism,[2] as persons whose behavior is other-directed rather than inner-directed,[3] and as a people whose educational institutions are dedicated to the cultivation of pliable, adaptable, conformity-seeking youth.[4]

THE MELTING POT AND CULTURAL DIVERSITY

Americans laud the melting pot ideology, which fosters belief in the desirability of a sameness and unity of national culture. This has been reflected in the traditional charge to the public schools to Americanize the children of foreigners so that they

[1] A *basic assumption* is a fundamental belief or a supposition that is taken for granted.

[2] William H. Whyte, Jr., *The Organization Man*, pp. 78–80, 143–52.

[3] David Riesman, Nathan Glazer, and Reuel Denney, *The Lonely Crowd*, pp. 37–38.

[4] Edgar Z. Friedenberg, *The Vanishing Adolescent*, p. 24.

will be absorbed into the cultural mainstream. Today this ideal is promoted in the American Southwest, for example, where the success in school of Hispano children is based on their fluency in English, not in Spanish. Yet Americans also laud the ideal of unity in diversity. A reflection of this belief is the charge to the schools to teach a genuine respect of cultural differences and an appreciation of the strengths found in the heterogeneous composition of our people.

THE STATUE OF LIBERTY AND NORDIC SUPERIORITY

Children memorize the stirring words of Emma Lazarus engraved at the base of the Statue of Liberty—words which preserve the promise of a national sanctuary for the "wretched refuse" from foreign shores. At the same time, America's highly restrictive immigration policies have carefully sustained the legacy of belief in Nordic superiority and the ideal of preserving pure, native American types.[5]

THE NATURE OF MAN

Americans hold varying beliefs concerning the fundamental nature of man: Some believe that man is basically a neutral creature and that his environment—particularly the educational environment—makes the individual whatever he is.[6] Others regard man as inherently sinful, evil. This doctrine, which has promoted harsh discipline theories regarding the education of the young and the ordering of human life in general, made a deep impact on American society through the New England Puritans. Others, in agreement with Konrad Lorenz,[7] view man as an aggressive animal whose naturally destructive impulses need to be channeled in socially positive directions. Others, heavily influenced by the ideas of biolog-

[5] John F. Kennedy, *A Nation of Immigrants*, pp. 101–11.

[6] E.g., see B. F. Skinner, *The Technology of Teaching*, pp. 9–28.

[7] Konrad Lorenz, *On Aggression*, pp. 266–90. See also Desmond Morris, *The Naked Ape*, and *The Human Zoo*.

ical evolution, chiefly those of Charles Darwin, see man as having no fixed nature whatsoever. Instead, the evolutionists regard man as part of the same on-going, progressive flux which is held to characterize the entire world. In this view, man is caught up in a developmental process of adaptation to constant change.[8] Still others view man as a fundamentally good and loving creature; the schools in this framework are conceived to be places where young people should learn the theory and practice of the loving human relationships which are believed to be in harmony with human nature.[9] Still others regard man as potentially good, the goodness being dependent upon the restoration of supernatural grace to the spiritually deprived individual. The ends of education, in the latter view, are that of elevating, regulating, and perfecting what the individual is inherently capable of becoming.[10]

Like American society as a whole, teachers also regard the phenomenon of human nature in very different ways. Consequently, whereas all teachers may believe that the names listed in their class registers belong to similar biological and psychological beings, the term "similar" has no uniform meaning to them. For example, it is possible that one teacher will see his students as a collection of active, willful, and stubborn creatures who will require firm control and utmost patience on his part. Another might see his students as passive, pliable units who must be shaped into a smooth, harmonious group under his instructional leadership. If the teacher believes that meas-

[8] E.g., see John Dewey, "The Influence of Darwinism on Philosophy," in *American Thought: Civil War to World War I*, ed. Perry Miller, pp. 214–25. See also Robert A. Nisbet, *Social Change and History: Aspects of the Western Theory of Development*. Nisbet argues that the Darwinian view of man and the associated ideas of human evolution, progress, and social development actually are based on Western beliefs which long preceded the publication of *The Origin of the Species*. See especially Nisbet's Chapter 5, "The Theory of Social Evolution," pp. 159–88.

[9] E.g., see M. F. Ashley Montagu, *The Direction of Human Development*, pp. 288–315.

[10] E.g., see Robert J. Henle, "A Roman Catholic View of Education," in *Philosophies of Education*, ed. Philip H. Phenix, pp. 75–83.

ured ability is the basis for the similarity of his students, he will see his class as composed of low ability, average, and high ability types. It is possible that another teacher will see class members as embryos of ideal men and women, and himself as an educational Pied Piper.

On the other hand, a teacher might be wary of emphasizing the similarities among his students. To him, human nature might imply no stereotyped formula at all. Thus he is likely to approach each new class without preconceived notions regarding the way his students should respond to him, to each other, and to the course content. Despite his fear and trembling in the face of every new unknown, such a teacher probably will find personal excitement and fresh professional challenges in encountering an infinite variety of human beings in his classes.

Personally, I am not sympathetic with views of students as stereotypes—either as miniatures of the teacher or as members of a clearly defined ability group. Nor do I agree with views of man as inherently passive and pliable, although I do believe that persons can be encouraged to live in this manner —a condition which I regard as a thwarting of human potential. Least of all am I in sympathy with views which hold that man is basically an evil, aggressive, and/or irrational creature, and that such impulses must be controlled and directed if man is not to destroy himself and others. Such a view seems to me to contain an inherent flaw: On one hand, man's basic nature is held to be evil, aggressive, and/or irrational. On the other hand, it is argued that man needs to be controlled and directed by *other* men, other men who by their very nature presumably would share the same negative impulses.

My own view approximates that of Carl Rogers—the belief that man's behavior is "exquisitely rational, moving with subtle and ordered complexity toward the goals his organism is endeavoring to achieve."[11] And I agree with Abraham Maslow, who writes:

[11] Carl R. Rogers, in *Perceiving, Behaving, Becoming,* prepared by the ASCD Yearbook Committee (Washington, D.C.: Association for Supervision and Curriculum Development, 1962), p. 83.

In the normal development of the normal child, it is now known that *most* of the time, if he is given a really free choice, he will choose what is good for his growth. This he does because it tastes good, feels good, gives pleasure or *delight*. This implies that *he* "knows" better than anyone else what is good for him.

Capacities clamor to be used, and cease their clamor only when they *are* well used. Not only is it fun to use our capacities, but it is also necessary. The unused capacity or organ can become a disease center or else atrophy, thus diminishing the person.

This force is one main aspect of the "will to health," the urge to grow, the pressure to self-actualization, the quest for one's identity. It is this that makes psychotherapy, education and self-improvement possible in principle.[12]

Capacities, I would emphasize, are just that—*capacities*. Healthy, satisfying, and growth-producing behavior on the part of a person is in no way guaranteed. An individual might do his choosing from a very circumscribed awareness of himself and others, and his choices might be limited to short-range self-gratification. Nonetheless, I believe that each individual has the option of making conscious decisions from a broad base of awareness and a long range of vision. The exercise of this option is precisely what I would like to nourish through the educative process.

As I see it, the view that man has an inherently positive nature, that he has a built-in thrust to actualize his potentialities, and that an adequate, healthy being is one who is functioning in harmony with his positive nature is compatible with the main lines of thought in Gestalt or cognitive-field psychology, existentialist philosophy, and Judeo-Christian humanism. In working with my own students, this particular network of ideas provides me with definite and distinctive answers to the fundamental questions, What is human nature? Who am I teaching? and Why am I teaching? *I regard the end goal of teaching as the autonomous functioning of unique individuals.*

[12] Abraham H. Maslow, in *Perceiving, Behaving, Becoming*, p. 83. See also Carl R. Rogers, *On Becoming a Person*, and Clark Moustakas, *Creativity and Conformity*.

1 at my responsibility to Comprehend.

Thus I share Ralph Harper's conviction that a teacher should aim to produce

> . . . not replicas, but men and women who stand apart from him even more distinctly than when he first met them . . . men and women who through their education have experienced the shock of discovering the infinite depths of the world and truth without giving up any of the partial truths they have encountered along the way. . . . A teacher knows that he has succeeded only when he has evidence that his pupils can hold something to be true that he himself is convinced is true, without having come to this truth by imitating the teacher, by reasoning, or by other powers of persuasion, including the persuasion of example. When one sees one's ideas quoted verbatim, one's heart should sink. But when one sees one's own ideas thought out anew as for the first time, then he is seeing the beginning of a free mind. The time will come soon enough when the liberated mind may go so far beyond the teacher's expressed thoughts that neither of them will see any overt connection between their ideas.[13]

But the reader should recognize that whereas I am deeply committed to an existentialist view of man, this particular orientation is one of many beliefs held by American educators. And, in all candor, mine is surely a minority viewpoint.

THE PROTESTANT WORK ETHIC AND
THE GRECO-ROMAN LEGACY

Another cherished principle found in the ideological core of American life is the Protestant work ethic. This principle has tended to sanctify manual labor for many Americans. The ideal is manifested in the Horatio Alger theme of pulling oneself up by the bootstraps. It is expressed through hard physical work in the home, on the farm, in the factory, in business— and in the unrelenting application to learning as a means of ensuring personal success.

[13] Ralph Harper, "Significance of Existence and Recognition for Education," in *Modern Philosophies and Education*, Fifty-fourth Yearbook of the National Society for the Study of Education, ed. Nelson B. Henry (Chicago: The University of Chicago Press, 1955), p. 237.

On the other hand, the classical Greco-Roman glorification of mental activity and a corresponding disdain for all manual labor have had an equally deep impact on American thought. Just as Plato accorded prestige to the thinking men over the working men in his ideal of the perfect society, Americans accord prestige to the white-collar worker and the professional person over the blue-collar worker. In this tradition, education is viewed as the road that will lead the individual away from a life of physical labor. Teachers operating from this orientation usually see their mission in terms of luring young people away from the prospects of a blue-collar future and into white-collar jobs (frequently with the likelihood of less income).

THE JEFFERSONIAN IDEAL AND
THE JACKSONIAN TRADITION

The elitist or Jeffersonian ideal of American public education holds that progress through the schools should be based on a student's meeting predetermined standards of excellence. This amounts to a winnowing-out process, in which the performance of a student is the decisive factor in determining whether he is promoted, is rerouted to a program requiring less ability, or is washed out of the system entirely. Although today this ideal is associated largely with the admission and promotion policies of colleges and universities, it is nonetheless applied in elementary and secondary school grading, promotion, and tracking policies. Exponents of the elitist doctrine regard education as an earned privilege.

By way of contrast, the egalitarian or Jacksonian concept of public education is based on flexible standards. It holds that the schools exist to meet the varying needs and demands of the American people. The comprehensive high school, in which a wide range of program offerings are supposed to correspond to the educational needs of all the youth in a community, is an ideal born of egalitarianism. Exponents of the egalitarian doctrine regard education as an inherent right of all citizens regardless of demonstrated ability.

DETERMINISM AND FREEDOM

Some Americans espouse the doctrine of determinism, which regards the individual's behavior as the result of all the external forces acting upon him. In such a framework, society as a whole is held totally responsible for the individual's behavior. Education, for the determinist, is a matter of reshaping and controlling the social environment, including the classroom environment, thereby conditioning the learner and inducing "engineered consent" to desired behavior patterns.[14]

Other Americans maintain the doctrine of absolute free will. Here the individual is regarded as having full responsibility for his actions over and beyond any possible environmental influences. This doctrine undergirds capital punishment laws across the nation. It is also expressed in views which see the high school dropout as the victim of his own negligence and irresponsibility. Once the learning opportunity has been provided by the teacher, it becomes the student's responsibility to exercise proper choice. Therefore, responsibility for success or failure in school resides finally with each student.

Still others maintain that at least three factors affect human behavior: heredity, environment, and a free or random element. Since the three factors operate in unknown degrees within each individual, it is held that final responsibility for each instance of human behavior and for success or failure in learning likewise remains an unknown. Although teachers operating from the latter point of view might teach as if all things depended upon environment (since that is the only factor of the three which lends itself to some degree of observation and control), nonetheless they would see each student as an ultimately indeterminate being insofar as what he actually will learn and how he actually will behave.

The age-old problem of free will versus determinism remains a significant issue, and it quite obviously affects the manner in which a teacher sees and works with any student. Caught up in a preoccupation with prediction and control of

[14] E.g., see B. F. Skinner, *Walden Two*, pp. 105, 291–92.

human behavior and influenced by the accompanying belief that all behavior is lawful and caused, many distinguished social scientists and educators accept determinism as the most feasible explanation of human actions.[15] Classroom teachers operating from a deterministic frame of reference are likely to establish models or norms of what student behavior and performance ought to be in any given situation. Test scores and other kinds of evidence collected from observable behavior thereupon serve as convenient indicators of whether environmental factors have been controlled sufficiently to produce the desired behavior patterns. B. F. Skinner probably has expressed more lucidly than anyone else the implications of deterministic learning theory. Through the character of Frazier in his 1948 novel, *Walden Two*, which describes a scientifically shaped Utopian society, Skinner announced, "Give me the specifications, and I'll give you the man! . . . Let us control the lives of our children and see what we can make of them."[16]

Whereas I do not underestimate the role of environmental factors in providing stimuli for thought and action, nor the role of environment in giving expression to chromosomes and genes, I am convinced that the rationale for a strict deterministic science of man has disappeared in the light of the *quantum theory*. First formulated by Max Planck,[17] the quantum theory thus far has had a very limited impact beyond the natural sciences. Its revolutionary implications for human intellectual history seemingly have been ignored by the vast majority of social scientists, despite the efforts of the brilliant Werner Heisenberg to push quantum mechanics into the realm of broader philosophic concerns:

[15] See, e.g., Donald Syngg and Arthur Combs, *Individual Behavior*, pp. 24–25. See also Skinner, *Walden Two*, pp. 105, 291–92; and Skinner, *The Technology of Teaching*, pp. 10, 171.

[16] B. F. Skinner, *Walden Two*, New York: The Macmillan Company, copyright, 1948, by B. F. Skinner; paperback Macmillan, 1962, p. 292.

[17] See Max Planck, "The Origin and Development of the Quantum Theory," *A Survey of Physics*, pp. 159–79.

Planck's theory has proved to be the key with which the door to the entire sphere of atomic physics could be opened. . . . With the mathematical formulation of quantum-theoretical laws *pure determinism had to be abandoned.* . . . The philosophic content of a science is only preserved *if science is conscious of its limits.* . . . Only by leaving open the question of the ultimate essence of a body, of matter, of energy, etc., can physics reach an understanding of the individual properties of the phenomena that we designate by these concepts, *an understanding which alone may lead us to real philosophical insight.* [Italics added.][18]

In brief, the world of atomic and subatomic nature as interpreted through quantum mechanics no longer has the strict mechanistic-materialist conception it enjoyed during the nineteenth century under the longtime influence of classical Newtonian physics. With quantum mechanics, all phenomena are removed from a rigorous determinism; nature functions instead only in terms of possibilities and tendencies. This means that we are able to predict only average, *not individual,* behavior. This is so, sometimes at least, because of "the factors introduced by either free or random elements, not simply because our data or our formulae are incomplete." In essence, quantum mechanics has caused the physicist to recognize that he cannot predict *anything* with exactness—that "the ultimate fact about the universe is not that everything in it obeys a law but that the random, or at least the unpredictable, is always present and effective."[19] Banesh Hoffmann has described the impact of quantum mechanics on the world of science:

Though now humbly confessing itself powerless to foretell the exact behavior of individual electrons, or photons, or other fundamental entities, [science] yet can tell with enormous confidence how

[18] Werner Heisenberg, *The Physicist's Conception of Nature,* trans. Arnold J. Pomerans (New York: Harcourt Brace Jovanovich, Inc., 1955), pp. 39, 180–81. See also Aage Petersen, *Quantum Physics and the Philosophical Tradition,* pp. 19–23.

[19] From *The Measure of Man,* copyright 1953, 1954, by Joseph Wood Krutch, reprinted by permission of the publishers, The Bobbs-Merrill Company, Inc., pp. 147–48.

organized = latitude.

such great multitudes of them must behave precisely. But for all this mass precision, we are only human if, on first hearing of the breakdown of determinacy in fundamental science, we look back longingly to the good old classical days, when waves were waves and particles particles, when the workings of nature could be readily visualized, and the future was predictable in every individual detail, at least in theory. But the good old days were not such happy days as nostalgic, rose-tinted retrospect would make them seem. Too many contradictions flourished unresolved. Too many well-attested facts played havoc with their pretensions. Those were but days of scientific childhood. There is no going back to them as they were. . . . As for the idea of strict causality, not only does science, after all these years, suddenly find it an unnecessary concept, it even demonstrates that according to the quantum theory strict causality is fundamentally and intrinsically undemonstrable. Therefore, strict causality is no longer a legitimate scientific concept, and must be cast out from the official domain of present-day science.[20]

The most formidable advancement of quantum mechanics has been expressed in Werner Heisenberg's famous *principle of uncertainty.* In Heisenberg's view, the quantum theory forces us to throw out the classical insistence (both in science and philosophy) that man can stand apart from the world he is observing in a detached, objective sense. Since man's system of questioning nature will affect his resulting description, *the very act of observing phenomena changes the description of the phenomena.* In the light of this interplay between nature and man, Heisenberg concluded that natural science is "made by man"—and as such is quite indeterminate.[21]

There are, it is true, many shades of opinion regarding the possible implications of the quantum theory. Most scientists rigorously confine their concerns to the microcosmic realm of physics and refrain from professional speculation beyond that point. Others, including nonscientists, have seen in these ideas

[20] From *The Strange Story of the Quantum* by Banesh Hoffmann, Dover Publications, Inc., New York, 1959, pp. 176–77, 179. Reprinted through permission of the publisher.

[21] Cf. Petersen, *Quantum Physics*, pp. 22–23.

which free our physical processes from strict causality a strong reinforcement for the existence of free will in ourselves.[22] Quite frankly, I stand with those who rejoice to find in the new ideas an analogue in the inanimate world to free will in human beings. If the random element of behavior is a factor that must be reckoned with in assessing the behavior of individual entities within the microcosmic world, then surely consideration must be given to the likelihood of a random element in the behavior of the larger, infinitely more complicated entities of the universe, including individual man.

To hold that freedom is an inalienable feature of human nature is not to say that it functions automatically. I believe that any individual, through conscious choice or through lack of self-awareness, can permit his behavior to be manipulated and controlled by others. However, instead of accepting the prevailing idea that "engineered consent" represents either the necessary or desirable way in which a life should be lived, I submit that a profound alternative needs to be explored as a vital part of the educative experience—*the idea that man is a freely choosing being.*

To phrase this idea more constructively, it is my belief that genes determine the limits of development under all environments, and that environments therefore should be provided which enable all human beings to attain their fullest development within those limits—the boundaries of which are forever beyond our ken. Further, I believe that the individual has the ability to respond to his environment actively and with an unknown, unpredictable measure of free choice. In my view, it is precisely this factor which affords an individual the opportunity of functioning in a personally responsible or irresponsible manner. That is to say, to whatever degree free choice is operating within an individual, I believe it is the distinguishing feature of his being human. To dismiss this random element of life on the grounds that it cannot be pinpointed and controlled seems to me to be shortsighted. It makes far more sense to develop in the educative process a recognition of this random element of behavior *so that an in-*

[22] Cf. discussions in Hoffmann, *Strange Story of the Quantum*, pp. 180–81, and Krutch, *Measure of Man*, pp. 140–158.

dividual will be encouraged to consider seriously the responsibilities appropriate to a free man.[23]

SOCIAL DARWINISM, CHARITY, AND WELFARISM

Another important belief that is part of the American ideological core is Social Darwinism. Dating from the nineteenth century, Social Darwinism fosters a survival-of-the-fittest approach to a highly competitive industrial society. Within this orientation extending help to the poor and unfit members of society is regarded as immoral or at least foolish.[24] The doctrine finds expression among those educators who regard American life in general as a competitive venture, and who therefore contend that competition should be the primary method of stimulating academic endeavor and of preparing students to cope with the realities of life.[25]

The same society has given rise to the doctrine of charity, or the "stewardship of the elite," which holds that social responsibility accompanies wealth.[26] Charity is a one-way process of rendering aid; it is conducted largely to mitigate human distress, not to change the conditions which cause it. In education, charity tends to promote the belief that those who are better educated have the right and the social re-

[23] The reader will find it profitable to compare Krutch's consideration of the quantum theory in *The Measure of Man* with the following existentialist discussions concerning free will, the unpredictability of behavior in a consciously choosing person, and the matter of assuming individual responsibility for this intrinsic freedom: *Existential Encounters for Teachers*, ed. Maxine Greene, pp. 103–4, 106; Viktor E. Frankl, *Man's Search for Meaning*, pp. 102–7, 157–58, 206–10; Gabriel Marcel, *Man against Mass Society*, pp. 13–25; Robert G. Olson, "The Human Condition," in *Modern Movements in Educational Philosophy*, ed. Van Cleve Morris, pp. 300–315; and Rollo May, *Love and Will*, pp. 196–204.

[24] E.g., see William Graham Sumner, "The Absurd Effort to Make the World Over," in *American Thought: Civil War to World War I*, ed. Perry Miller, pp. 92–104.

[25] E.g., see Giles F. Liegerot, "Is Academic Competition for You?" pp. 148–52.

[26] E.g., see Andrew Carnegie, *The Gospel of Wealth*.

sponsibility to make decisions for all those persons who have less education; it also sustains the belief that there is no necessary correlation between economic well-being and educational success.

Since the national institutionalization of the welfare-state doctrine in 1933, Americans have widely proclaimed this doctrine also. Here rehabilitative assistance to individual members is regarded as the responsibility of the larger society. The myriad War-on-Poverty efforts, the National Defense Education Act programs, and the Nixon administration's proposal for a minimum guaranteed income all express the mutual obligations involved in the welfare ideal—that society helps all individuals, who in turn are expected somehow to return the results of that assistance to society and to become fully participating members thereof.

NATIONALISM AND THE NUREMBERG DOCTRINE

Finally, American youth are imbued with the doctrine of nationalism, which encourages loyalty to a given geographic unit, namely, one's country. In this doctrine, values and morality tend to follow the flag, and, for all practical purposes, young people are taught the ideal of Commodore Stephen Decatur, "Our Country! In her intercourse with foreign nations may she always be in the right; but our country, right or wrong."

However, distinguished Americans were prominent in the War Crimes Trials of 1945 and in the formulation of the Nuremberg Doctrine, which is predicated on the belief in a higher morality, a morality held to be more binding than national interests. To say the least, the doctrines of nationalism and Nuremberg pose critical questions in terms of what the schools should teach the young about morality. The teacher who blithely envisions that his curriculum specialty will be a good means of demonstrating to his students the "soundness of the principles on which our nation was founded" needs to develop acute sensitivity to the volatile ideas with which he is dealing.

I recall a particularly uncomfortable incident which pointed up my own naïveté in coping with the conflict which often exists between national and international morality. During the era of the first manned orbital flights, I faithfully sought to convey to my high school social studies students the popular notion that before we sent the first man into space, we made certain he was going to come back safely since we Americans value a single human life even above a space victory over the Russians. Usually students would accept such a statement without openly questioning its validity. But on one occasion, an outspoken young fellow broke the respectful pause which followed my pronouncement with: "Oh? Well, my brother just came home from the Marines. And he was telling us that they showed him how to fix his bayonet on his rifle and then run down a field and stick it deep into the guts of a dummy. It made him sorta sick, but they told him to forget that the dummy was supposed to be a human being!" My student, of course, had pointed up the most agonizing moral issue of all time—the problem of war.[27]

Although the above ideas represent only a sampling of our ideological core, they illustrate that Americans as a whole believe in

. . . a mass of contradictory statements, half of which cancel out the other half, and all of which add up to the most confused set of ideals that any mighty nation has fallen heir to in the history of the world.[28]

[27] Cf. implications of the revealing exposé of Marine brutality against fellow Marines: Jack Fincher, "The Hog-Tied Brig Rats of Camp Pendleton," pp. 32–37. Consider also the ethical problems posed by the mysterious case of the Green Berets: Frank McCullock, "The Fall of a 'Lost Soldier,'" pp. 17–19; also "The Massacre at Mylai," pp. 36–45. See also Robert J. Lifton, "Beyond Atrocity," pp. 23–25, 54.

[28] Sidney J. Harris, *Majority of One*, p. 85. See also "American Society and Values," in *Readings in the Socio-Cultural Foundations of Education*, ed. John H. Chilcott, Norman C. Greenberg, and Herbert B. Wilson, pp. 162–221.

Quite obviously, the American way of life represents many cleavages in thought. And the teacher who plunges into his career with the idea of passing on to his students a harmonious national synthesis of "the good life" is going to have an extremely difficult chore. It is simply not possible for anyone to subscribe *without internal conflict* to all the ideas and beliefs embedded in the foundational level of American life— nor to subscribe to all of them with equal fervor.

CONTROVERSY IN THE CLASSROOM

The conflict in basic societal goals and values can pose difficulties for the teacher not only in terms of *where* he intends to go in the classroom but of *what content* he will select to achieve his purposes. Recently I conferred with a student teacher on a serious problem he had encountered in his sophomore world history class. He had developed a fine unit of study on the origin of man. His purpose was to promote among his students an understanding of the numerous views on the origin of man and an appreciation of those viewpoints differing from their own. He related to me how many of his students had been hostile to the introduction of ideas about evolution. "They are strong fundamentalists," he commented, "and are quite close-minded about the whole matter. How do you combat this close-mindedness without wrecking their faith?"

We thereupon examined the line of questioning which he had used in introducing the unit content. First, he had elicited from them the three main ways in which men have claimed to know: revelation, reason, and sensory experience. Developing the theme of the need in a democratic society to listen to other people's ideas, he included the following questions to get his students to think about the ideas they held: "Can we ever know anything for sure? Isn't there a chance that your ideas are wrong? Even if you believe God's word has been revealed to you, isn't there a chance you have misinterpreted it since human beings aren't perfect like God?" He summarized the lesson with the statement, "Our ideals of freedom of speech and intellectual freedom are based on the assumption that if you let ideas come out freely and in great numbers, this will somehow help us get closer to the 'Truth.' "

Since this young man's ostensible purpose was to create a greater openness in the thinking of his students, I asked him to consider the extent of the openness fostered by the content he had selected. "What might have been the impact on your students," I asked, "if you had also considered the different kinds of proofs associated with the three ways of acquiring knowledge? How might they have responded to the idea that validity needs to be understood *in relationship to the system of knowledge employed;* for example, that the empirical verification required for knowledge gained through sensory experience is actually *irrelevant* as proof in the highly personal, mystical, and/or intuitive acquisition of knowledge through revelation? And," I further asked, "what might have been the students' reactions if you had used the question regarding the certainty of our knowledge to introduce content to explain the absolute-relative continuum of ideas that men of integrity can and do hold, and how these beliefs are related to still other ideas that men hold about the nature of the world and values?"

In effect, I attempted to point out to this student teacher that he had developed content which subtly sought to lead students down the primrose path to the idea of tentative, emerging truths and that such a path was threatening to students committed to the validity of unchanging, universal truths. He had given many of his students no basis of support for their own ideas, and against the threat of having their own cherished beliefs undermined, those students did precisely what any students can be expected to do—they closed their minds even more firmly against the intrusion of disturbing new ideas.

At the end of our conference the student teacher decided that the only way he could hope to develop an openness in his students was to create a classroom atmosphere wherein each student would feel that his ideas *were* going to be respected whatever other ideas might be introduced. Such an atmosphere could be created only by a deliberately broad selection of content and a treatment of that content in such a way that the student would realize the significance of basic assumptions in *his* life regarding goal and value formation, and also realize that the final choice of what is best is truly up to him.

In searching for a way in which he might create such a climate, the student teacher decided that his students actually had given him the opening he needed. During the preceding stormy class session, one of the hostile students had flatly declared, "I don't think we should talk about controversial ideas like evolution in here!" Another student had quickly supported the closure of controversial topics by insisting that "everyone should be allowed to do his own thing!" The student teacher decided to build several class sessions around the idea of controversy itself.

The following day he opened the class by recalling the students' comments about controversy. He suggested that their comments were important and that they were worthy of serious exploration. "Why," he asked his class, "isn't it a good idea for us to talk about controversial topics?" In a spirited discussion, many members of his class conveyed their feelings that such topics are unfair because discussions about them always offend someone, and that furthermore if someone believes something is true without a doubt, there is no sense in talking about it any further.

With that, the student teacher asked the class to see if they could agree on a definition of controversy. After considerable discussion and after referring to the dictionary, the class decided that controversy is a dispute or lack of agreement concerning any matter of opinion. Next, the student teacher made a follow-up assignment. He asked each member of the class to survey the mass media and any other reference material of his choice, and to bring to class at least three topics which he felt were beyond controversy. These topics, the teacher explained, would then be considered by the full class as a possible basis for the course content.

Over the next several days, each of the topics submitted by the students was examined by the class against the question,

Is this topic beyond controversy? As they tested one another's ideas, they came to the conclusion that all matters of any consequence in human life are controversial. "If controversy seems to be a part of everything we could conceivably talk about in here," interjected the student teacher at this point, "isn't our only alternative not to talk about anything at all? If this is the case," he continued, "how then should we go about conducting our affairs in a democratic society, in which action is based on the expectation that we will be able to deliberate with each other?" Against these prodding questions, the class explored other alternatives, ultimately deciding that the crux of the whole matter is the *attitude* with which people approach controversy, that deliberation depends on whether or not differing opinions can be respected, and that majority opinion in a democracy does not automatically mean the *best* opinion.

At the end of this series of class meetings, the student teacher was well on his way toward achieving his purpose, and in the process he had removed the cause of student hostility and close-mindedness.

As the preceding case illustrates, a simplistic "transmission of American core values" is well nigh impossible within a pluralistic society and within schools which presumably serve that total society. The student teacher found it advantageous to incorporate a discussion of the nature of controversy itself into his curriculum content—to help his students become comfortable in the face of a multiplicity of human values and goals. However, an open recognition of the nature of controversy is not the most popular means of coping with our core values. Many teachers, administrators, parents, and school board members regard controversy as dangerous for two reasons: their belief in the immaturity of young minds and their fear of possible censure from the larger community.

We will return to this matter of controversy after examining alternative ways of establishing a foundation for American education.

CHAPTER THREE

A FOUNDATION:
SOME ALTERNATIVES

From time to time national educational organizations have
tried to provide a foundation for the development of curricula
by formulating statements of major purposes and goals that
represent a consensus. Although American education is a
highly decentralized structure as far as ultimate decision-
making is concerned, these national statements have served
as models for the formulation of local-district educational
goals. One of the best-known statements of purpose was is-
sued in 1918 by the Commission on the Reorganization of
Secondary Education. At that time the commission outlined
seven cardinal objectives for secondary schools: health, command of fundamental processes, worthy home membership,
vocational competence, effective citizenship, worthy use of
leisure, and ethical character.[1] Similar objectives were presented by national organizations in 1938,[2] 1944,[3] and 1954.[4]

[1] U.S. Commission on the Reorganization of Secondary Education,
Cardinal Principles of Secondary Education.

Collectively, the above objectives have long been regarded as an expression of national thinking regarding the function of schools and the specific tasks of educators. Obviously these statements have been taken seriously by generations of American teachers, who faithfully have reproduced variations of them in their curriculum guides. Not so obvious, however, is the Alice-in-Wonderland quality of these statements of purpose—that is, the words are likely to mean anything people want them to mean. The confusion which surrounds the implementation of such statements can be understood when one realizes that the consensus they reflect has been achieved at a highly abstract level. Unfortunately, these efforts to achieve verbal agreement on educational goals have promoted the practice of giving lip service to the stock words and phrases that describe the goals, in the belief that everyone interprets them the same. In reality the classroom teacher is confronted with a set of glittering generalities which presumably serve as guidelines for teaching.

EDUCATION FOR ETHICAL CHARACTER

To illustrate the problem at hand: What precisely does the directive regarding ethical character mean to the classroom teacher? Does it mean that he should prescribe attitudes, behaviors, and beliefs to his students? If so, what are the criteria for such a task—and how and by whom are they determined? Should the teacher, for example, explain to his students that ethical character develops through adherence to the eternal Mosaic Law, and that this represents a fixed system of rules and truths which must be learned and accepted by the student

---

[2] NEA Educational Policies Commission, *The Purposes of Education in American Democracy.*

[3] NEA Educational Policies Commission, *Education for All American Youth.*

[4] NEA Educational Policies Commission, *Education for All American Youth: A Further Look.*

if he is to live the good life? Should the teacher, instead, explain to his students that ethical codes and the good life grow out of the changing needs of society as a whole, and that since there is no fixed system of behavior, students must learn to evaluate what is good and what is bad in terms of the observable consequences of behavior on human lives? Should the teacher explain that the greatest good for the greatest number is the best criterion of ethical behavior? Or should he, as Ralph Harper suggests,[5] explain that the quest for truth must be disassociated from majority opinion, and that although the good life necessitates cooperative living, the particular attributes of ethical character remain the prerogative of each individual even if he is the only one to hold such beliefs? And how, specifically, should the teacher go about explaining and how should the student go about learning ethical behavior? Should it be through a process of exhortation and imposition? Should it be through example and emulation? Or should it be through exposition and self-determination?

Personally, I see the teacher's task essentially as that of giving the student free rein to determine for himself what it means to live morally—in terms of the self and in terms of the self in relationship to other people. It might be argued that to give a student free rein—in effect, to permit him to stand apart from the teacher—is to invite moral and social chaos. However, in view of my assumption that man is basically a positive, potentially responsible creature, I regard the emergence of a destructive social climate as a remote possibility— if the student is truly afforded the opportunity of choosing his own ethical code. In any event, this is a risk that I am willing to assume in the face of a greater one—namely, the risk that *moral apathy* will be fostered by the policy of insisting that a student make a specific set of predetermined, authoritarian givens a part of his own life. This is a practice, in my opinion, which tends to ensure that externally imposed codes will *remain* external to the individual.

[5] Ralph Harper, "Significance of Existence and Recognition for Education," in *Modern Philosophies and Education*, ed. Nelson B. Henry, pp. 237–38, 249.

However, my humanistic concerns for moral development should not be equated with permissiveness. Nor should my comments in this matter of teaching for ethical character be mistaken for an espousal of total relative or situational ethics. Although there are some values which I do hold as conditional to a given time, place, and circumstance, there are others which I regard as unconditional and universal[6] in nature. In the latter case, I recognize the necessity of interpreting and reinterpreting universals within the subjective framework of a constantly changing physical realm of reality. Also, in admitting to a transempirical leap of faith, I would emphasize three points: First, my ethical code represents a self-examined set of values; I have freely chosen them as my own. Second, despite my espousal of universals, I neither expect nor desire that all other individuals adopt my particular moral code, even of their own accord. Third, since my espousal of universals is a conscious leap of faith—and hence is humbled by the doubts, risks, and ultimate uncertainties which accompany any such leap—I rigorously oppose an authoritarian imposition of these values on other persons. And I oppose authoritarian imposition *whatever* the age, experience, and educational level of students.

My particular interpretation of ethical behavior is, of course, not the prevailing point of view. Judging from our teaching practices, more educators than not seem to hold the classical view that the human being needs to have a basic set of values and beliefs inculcated during the "formative" stages of his development. After the individual reaches a designated stage of emotional and intellectual maturation, he is regarded as someone who has been properly equipped to make independent value judgments. If the reader shares this view of what it means to educate for ethical behavior, then his chief task will be to determine the proper body of values and beliefs to be inculcated, and to ascertain the precise time at which a student is mature enough to be encouraged to think

[6] Philosophically, universals are ideas that are regarded as trans-empirically located, permanent, and unchanging. They are the antithesis of man-made, constantly changing, "emerging" values.

independently. Aristotle, for example, believed that a student should be carefully nurtured, guided, and inculcated with proper values and beliefs until he reached the age of twenty-one. Given this particular chronology, methods for promoting independent thinking in students would lie quite beyond the realm of concerns of the contemporary public school teacher.

THE CENTRAL PURPOSE OF AMERICAN EDUCATION

The Educational Policies Commission of the National Education Association recognized some of the serious shortcomings inherent in the previously stated educational goals. Hence in 1961 they published *The Central Purpose of American Education*, which addressed itself to filling the need for a single, comprehensive principle which would "enable the school to identify its necessary and appropriate contributions to individual development and the needs of society."[7] The principle identified was *the development of the rational powers of man*. The commission explained that these powers involved "recalling and imagining, classifying and generalizing, comparing and evaluating, analyzing and synthesizing, and deducing and inferring."[8] It further claimed that such processes would "enable one to apply logic and the available evidence to his ideas, attitudes, and actions, and to pursue better whatever goals he may have."[9] Since development of the rational powers was offered as a means of consolidating and making more meaningful the earlier stated cardinal principles and the subsequent national attempts for a consensus of educational purpose, it warrants careful attention.

The Educational Policies Commission's obvious intention was that the goal of developing the student's rational powers would provide the teacher with a practical guideline for selecting, implementing, and evaluating curriculum content.

[7] Educational Policies Commission, *The Central Purpose of American Education* (Washington: National Education Association, 1961), p. 2. (The EDC is now defunct, but the NEA still has this publication in stock.)

[8] *Ibid.*, p. 5.

[9] *Ibid.*

However, implicit in the stated goal is the assumption that *something specific* will be recalled, imagined, classified, generalized, compared, evaluated, analyzed, synthesized, deduced, and inferred. For example, one cannot advise the teacher to help his students recall without considering the nature of what is to be recalled. To do otherwise would be akin to operating in a theoretical vacuum. Here is the crux of the difficulty and precisely the point where this more recent attempt at consensus breaks down: the possible in-depth meanings of the word "rationality."

EXPERIMENTALISM AND RATIONAL THINKING

If a teacher is oriented to a *pragmatist* or *experimentalist* view of the world, and thereby delimits himself to a reality, to knowledge, and to values which are verifiable through sensory experience, he will define what it means to be rational within those boundaries. Specifically, he will teach and will encourage his students to learn as if all problems of knowledge can and should be handled within the reflective method.[10] Whatever the particular phraseology employed by various experimentalists, the reflective method of inquiry tends to follow five steps: (1) The individual becomes aware of a problem when confronted with a difficulty of some kind. (2) He clarifies the problem, inductively[11] arriving at possible solutions by observing relevant sensory data. (3) He formulates a definite supposition or hypothesis, deducing[12] the implications of his limited observations so that his hypothesis can be tested

[10] E.g., see John Dewey, *How We Think*, pp. 106–18; see also George G. Geiger, *Philosophy and the Social Order*, pp. 102–52.

[11] Inductive reasoning or form of logic moves from an analysis of particular instances in the same category to generalizations which are derived from those particulars. (E.g.: Tom, Dave, and John were admitted to the basketball game after presenting their student ID cards at the ticket booth. Therefore, I can infer that Mike, who is now presenting his ID card, will also be admitted.)

[12] Deductive reasoning or form of logic moves from a general statement to a particular instance. (E.g.: All students will be admitted to the basketball game. Mike is a student. Therefore, I can infer that Mike will be admitted.)

in other observable situations. (4) He elaborates his knowledge of the problem by collecting and examining additional data. (5) He tests his hypothesis by overt action of some kind, and draws his conclusions on the basis of the evidence examined, supporting, altering, or rejecting his original hypothesis. In any event, his resulting conclusions are held with varying degrees of tentativity, instead of certitude, in the anticipation that new data might come to light which would necessitate further revision of his findings.[13] To the experimentalist, this process of thinking is the *only* logical and intelligent way to think about anything.

An experimentalist teacher is also likely to place a high premium on curriculum activities in which students learn from direct experience. For example, a science teacher in developing a unit of study on the conservation of natural resources might have his students make a number of field trips to observe firsthand how the community park system is planned and operated, how the water system functions, and how industrial air pollution is handled. Following the initial exposure of students to conservation problems as they actually exist, the teacher might have his class theoretically attempt to solve those problems. At this point, the students could begin to collect data on man's attempts to cope with such problems to date (for example, by seeking information from United States Department of Interior agencies, state and local agencies, and scientific treatises). On the basis of the empirical evidence collected and examined, the class then might seek to arrive at some definite recommendations on ways in which their community could conserve its natural resources. Ideally these recommendations would be tested beyond the science class itself, and the students would be given an opportunity to submit their proposals, for example, to the City Planning Commission for review.[14]

[13] See Dewey, *How We Think*, pp. 106–18; see also Morris L. Bigge and Maurice P. Hunt, "What Is the Reflective Method?" *Psychological Foundations of Education*, pp. 307–11.

[14] Cf. H. Gordon Hullfish, "An Experimentalist View of Education," in *Philosophies of Education*, ed. Philip H. Phenix, pp. 9–24.

In this approach to learning, the teacher would have limited interest in guiding his students toward specifically desired conclusions. He would attempt to gear all activities so that his students would become involved in the *processes* of recalling and imagining, classifying and generalizing, comparing and evaluating, analyzing and synthesizing, and deducing and inferring from empirical evidence examined by the reflective method. And his evaluation of their success would be based on their demonstrated skill in utilizing these processes to arrive at operational conclusions regarding the problem—conclusions which the students would be expected to defend in terms of the supporting evidence. Within the experimentalist framework of thinking, for students to engage in recalling and imagining, classifying and generalizing, comparing and evaluating, analyzing and synthesizing, and deducing and inferring from evidence *beyond* the empirically verifiable world of reality would be regarded as an irrational approach to knowledge.[15]

TRANSEMPIRICISM AND RATIONAL THINKING

On the other hand, to a teacher who holds that a realm of reality, knowledge, and values exists *beyond* that of the empirical world, the recalling, imagining, classifying, etc., of something beyond the boundaries of the empirical world is considered as the *highest* and most desirable exercise of rational thought. Although such a teacher might employ the reflective method of inquiry in some instances, he would regard it as inadequate in getting at the most important domain of knowledge. For him, rationality implies a belief in the inherent ability of the human mind to transcend sensory

[15] Despite experimentalists' overwhelming emphasis on visible and empirically verifiable evidence, it should be noted that they do not test mathematical ideas in experience. These are regarded as analytic assertions and are legitimately part of rational knowledge. This is also true of esthetics, although experimentalists do regard some aspects of esthetics as testable in experience. (See a reflection of this in the John Dewey quotation from *Art as Experience* which appears on p. 84.)

experience and to apprehend certain self-evident, universal, permanent, unchanging principles, ideas, and truths. Such a teacher, for example, might encourage students to develop their mental capacities so that the "self-evident truths" embodied in the Declaration of Independence will be manifested to them as they were to Thomas Jefferson—that is, through an operation of the intellect that does not depend on empirical evidence for verification.[16]

In this orientation, rational powers are understood to be those powers common to every human being by virtue of his human nature—although the powers tend to vary in degree in different individuals, thereby giving rise to Jefferson's "natural aristocracy of talent" and to Plato's hierarchy of intelligence: the men of gold, silver, and brass. These mental powers enable the individual to acquire and use knowledge that is regarded as common to all men in all times and in all places.[17]

A teacher who is transempirically oriented would seek to engage his students in a search for ideas which he regards as existing in fixed patterns, and he is likely to hold that such a search can be conducted at a largely theoretical level and within the confines of the classroom itself.[18] A mathematics teacher, for example, might structure his course in geometry around a fixed, axiomatic Euclidean basis. Through lecture, demonstration, discussion, and the working of geometric exercises by his students, he would seek to lead those students toward an understanding of certain fixed ideas in mathematics. His evaluation of their success would be based on their demonstrated achievement in apprehending what he regards as pervasive mathematical truths. Learning, in this framework, is essentially a matter of storing the student's memory with

[16] Adrienne Koch and William Peden, *The Life and Selected Writings of Thomas Jefferson*, pp. 316, 318–19.

[17] E.g., see Harry S. Broudy, "A Classical Realist View of Education," in *Philosophies of Education*, ed. Philip H. Phenix, p. 20. See also Robert Maynard Hutchins, *The Higher Learning in America*, p. 66.

[18] Harry S. Broudy, "A Classical Realist View of Education," pp. 21–22.

all things which the teacher deems necessary for an intelligent person to possess, whether those things are

. . . sentences great men have spoken—poems or parts of poems, and passages of prose—along with pieces of powerful music, glimpses of powerful painting, classical formulas in mathematics, chemistry, and physics, and the patterns of certain instruments without which science is helpless.[19]

What a transempirical teacher might consider an exercise of rationality is further complicated by the classical Platonic and Aristotelian dispute over the significance of the sensory world in the total scheme of acquiring knowledge and also over the *location* of the knowledge available to man.

Plato held that the sensory world is a highly illusory world, and that consequently rationality involves the act of mentally removing oneself from the sensory world, which he deemed quite insignificant, and engaging in pure intellectual activity. Plato further believed that universal ideas do not exist in the world of space and time but are *innate* to man. It was the teacher's function, therefore, not to impart external ideas to the learner but to serve as a midwife in drawing out ideas that were already implanted within the student as an inherent aspect of his humanness.

Plato advocated four primary methods to put the learner in touch with knowledge that was already his, although in an unrecognized stage of development: (1) exhortation by the teacher, thereby jolting the student into a state of anxiety about himself; (2) Socratic conversation, in which the teacher —through a series of pointed questions and comments—led the student to discover precisely the truths which the teacher wanted him to discover; (3) reinforcement by the teacher of certain behaviors and punishment of others, thereby conditioning the student to desire what the teacher deemed he ought to desire and to dislike what it was deemed he should

[19] Mark Van Doren, *Liberal Education*, © Mark Van Doren, 1943, original publication Henry Holt and Co.; paperback Beacon Press, 1959, pp. 95–96.

dislike; and (4) training of the student in abstract mathematical speculation, through which the learner would be able to intuit the ultimate scheme of reality itself.[20]

Aristotle also held to the existence of a realm of unchanging universals beyond the spacio-temporal world; however, he did not find such knowledge innate to man. Nor did he regard the sensory world illusory; in fact, he argued that higher mental activity is not possible without prior sensory stimulation. So instead of negating the value of sensory data as had his teacher, Plato, Aristotle held that data inductively derived from the experiential world is necessary in the learning process to trigger the mind's capacity to ascertain universal premises. Unlike Plato's reliance on intuitive forms of reasoning or inner reflection as a means of drawing out knowledge from within, Aristotle relied on a more formal method of deductive reasoning known as syllogistic logic. Through this method, he sought to apprehend knowledge that he viewed as *external* to man; and this theoretical construct provided a means of proceeding from knowledge to knowledge without subjecting the truth of that knowledge to empirical verification.[21] Instead, the test of truth in syllogistic reasoning is the internal consistency of the major and minor premises; if the premises are consistent with one another, the individual arrives at a logically necessary truth and can hold this truth with the same certitude with which he holds his initial premise.

To illustrate Aristotle's method of reasoning: An individual in surveying the empirical world of everyday affairs could inductively derive data to the effect that his fellow human beings tend to die. Such sensory data, according to Aristotle, could trigger off the mind's capacity to apprehend the universal truth that all men are mortal, which would thereupon be accepted as the major premise. Then if a subsequent minor premise of a more specific nature (Socrates is a man) is in-

[20] Harry S. Broudy and John R. Palmer, *Exemplars of Teaching Method*, pp. 31–46.

[21] Renford Bambrough, *The Philosophy of Aristotle*, pp. 40–41, 137–59.

ternally related to the major premise, the inevitable conclusion follows that Socrates is mortal. Here the validity of the conclusion depends upon the relationship between the statements of the syllogism, *not* upon the relationship between the statements and sensory evidence.

The thing to grasp here is that it is possible to be logically true without being empirically true. For example, a teacher who goes through the following syllogistic form of rational thinking starts with an erroneous premise but nonetheless arrives at a logically necessary conclusion: "Negro persons are inferior in intelligence to Caucasian persons. I have a Negro student in my class. Therefore, the Negro can be expected to perform at a much lower level than my Caucasian students." However, the validity of this line of reasoning can be judged only in terms of its internal consistency—that is, on the basis of the relationship between the statements of the syllogism itself; its validity or invalidity is not properly ascertained in terms of empirical data. What needs to be recognized in the above illustration is that although empirical data can conceivably be used as a negative or positive support for the major and minor premises and for the logical conclusion derived therefrom, more typically this form of reasoning is used to get at transempirical knowledge which does *not* lend itself to material verification. A case in point is the kinds of self-evident truths about which Jefferson wrote in the Declaration of Independence; there is no conceivable way of subjecting the nature and substance of such knowledge to laboratory analysis. Therefore, the crux of the syllogistic method of reasoning is the acceptance of one's initial premise *as if it were unequivocally true*. With acceptance of the major premise, the individual thereby provides a means of getting at logically necessary kinds of knowledge.

Although the Platonic and Aristotelian thought sketched here go back in origin more than two thousand years, it should be noted that both philosophers gave rise to powerful lines of reasoning which have been carried down through Western civilization to the present day. And although there have been many variations of neo-Platonism (or philosophical *idealism*) and as many variations of neo-Aristotelianism (or philosophical *realism*), the main lines of thought and the subsequent educational implications have remained remarkably constant. More alike than different in their basic assumptions, idealists and realists are also more alike than different in the educational goals which they promote and in the teaching methodology which they employ to achieve those goals. Together, idealism and realism have provided the backbone of Western education, constituting what is frequently referred to as traditional education, wherein the teacher assumes that there is an existing body of essential knowledge which the student must learn in order to think well and to live well, and that the teacher's role is to put the student in touch with such knowledge.[22] In both branches of traditional education, the teacher places considerable emphasis on the study of mankind's accumulated records (for example, the *Great Books*) as repositories of great and enduring knowledge from all ages and as models of excellence which are forever relevant.

EXISTENTIALISM AND RATIONAL THINKING

A teacher who functions from an *existentialist* orientation is likely to regard all the above approaches to rational thinking with a somewhat jaundiced eye. To him, the philosophies of experimentalism, realism, and idealism all place a high premium on a kind of objectivity in which the learner is cast in a spectator role and is encouraged to stand back from ideas and/or problems as an impersonal analyst.[23] The existentialist is extremely critical of the spectator approach to knowledge

[22] The instructional role within this broad framework tends to be quite consistent whether the "teacher" is in the traditional form of a person or in the newer mode of an exotic machine. Compare, for example, the conventional teaching agency described throughout Jacques Barzun's *Teacher in America,* and the mechanized teaching agency proposed in George B. Leonard's *Education and Ecstasy,* pp. 139–55.

[23] For a detailed explanation of the spectator role in relationship to existentialist philosophy, see Appendix A.

on two counts. He holds (1) that no individual can ever get outside his own skin—that his perceptions of reality always are deeply colored by himself;[24] and (2) that unless an individual can grapple with problems as one who is involved with them with his whole being, then knowledge—however interesting—will make no real difference in his life. Rationality, for the existentialist, is an exercise of the intellect *coupled with intense personal feeling.* Therefore, such a teacher attempts to involve his students subjectively in matters of vital concern to them as individuals. A key method is *intellectual confrontation,* wherein the teacher attempts to stir up his students by focusing attention on ethical problems in which they have a personal stake. At every opportunity, the teacher seeks to expose students to disturbing, incompatible, and uncomfortable ideas. In other words, he deliberately tries to foment a constructive kind of mental anxiety, or *disquietude* —a learning atmosphere in which intellectual and emotional complacency is well-nigh impossible.

For example, a teacher operating from an existential point of view might have his students evaluate the quality of human life in the twentieth century. In order to get at a feeling level for the significance of life per se, the teacher first might seek to heighten his students' consciousness of death. He might introduce the study by examining these themes as depicted in various literary works and by considering specific instances which treat life-and-death issues in present society as a whole. He probably would share his own concerns and feelings with his students but ultimately would encourage them to grapple with life and death at a level of personal significance. George Kneller has suggested that an existentialist teacher could encourage students to live more authentically through an awareness of their own deaths. He points out that

[24] The characteristic subjectivity of existentialist philosophy, it seems to me, is highly compatible with the general intellectual outlook of quantum mechanics, particularly in terms of the interplay between nature and man as advanced by Werner Heisenberg's *principle of uncertainty* (see Chapter 2, p. 33).

. . . it is only the thought of death which makes us truly aware of the values of life. To be conscious of death—our own death—is not to surrender to morbidity but to make possible the enhancement of living. The student should be shown that existence for its own sake does not override all other values, and that it is actually possible to pay too high a price for the privilege of remaining alive. Often it may be finer to die for an ideal than, by preserving one's life, to betray one. History shines with examples of those who willingly made the supreme sacrifice, of mothers who died for their children, soldiers for their country, martyrs for their faith. "Greater love than this hath no man shown, that he laid down his life for a friend." Indeed, the student has before him two magnificent examples, which eclipse all others—of Christ in His agony dying for the redemption of mankind, and of Socrates taking the hemlock, that the rule of law in Athens might be upheld.

Although the teacher should inspire his pupils by describing such examples, his task does not end there. By making them aware of the inevitability and, on occasions even, the desirability of death, he should lead them to examine the quality of their own lives, for the imminence of death is the most potent spur to self-examination. On the other hand, the teacher would be ill-advised to persuade the student that he lives under perpetual sentence of death, although in the existentialist sense this may be true. Rather, the student must learn to live his life in the knowledge that some day, a day like this one, life is going to end. Then let him ask himself what he is living for. Is he living to the full as a free man, or is he content simply to exist? When he dies, will it have mattered whether he lived at all? Let him recall the words of Blaise Pascal, "Live today as if you were to die tomorrow."[25]

As Kneller indicates in the above passage, to have students consider the significance of death is to foster not morbidity or emotionalism but more creative, self-directed living. His point recalls a teaching experience I had in 1960. The Hungarian Revolution was still a fresh cataclysmic event on the world scene and a timely topic for consideration by my high school social studies students. One day we viewed a dramatic film

[25] George F. Kneller, *Introduction to the Philosophy of Education* (New York: John Wiley & Sons, Inc., 1964), pp. 60–61. See also *Existential Encounters for Teachers*, ed. Maxine Greene, pp. 26–27.

which depicted the bloody, unsuccessful struggle on the streets of Budapest. Of all the violence and stirring narrative in that film, the scene that made the deepest impact on my students concerned a fifteen-year-old Hungarian girl who had flung herself inside a Russian tank as a human grenade. That girl was their peer, and precisely because my students felt a kinship with her, the girl's fate had a profound effect on their own thinking. That film provoked among a group of young Americans a rich, memorable discussion about the quality of human life and about values which they personally would be willing to live and die by.

RATIONALITY AND THE SCIENTIFIC METHOD

Further complicating the possible meanings of rational thinking is the relationship of rational powers to the scientific method of inquiry. It is a rare teacher who is not touched by the dominant force of science in twentieth-century America. A random survey among contemporary teachers would undoubtedly reveal that the overwhelming majority are convinced they are approaching their subject matter in a scientific way and are helping their students acquire a scientific perspective on their particular field. But would these teachers mean the same thing when they employed that popular phrase "the scientific method"?

If a teacher is an experimentalist, he equates the process of reflective thinking with the scientific method.[26] To him, the task of teaching a student to think scientifically means to create a habit of mind in which the student will apply the five steps of reflective thinking as he encounters all aspects of human life—from ordinary experiences to profound problems. Scientific thinking to the experimentalist is the process of subjecting all knowledge to constant critical analysis and empirical verification. Although he undoubtedly will have a deep respect for the pinnacles of human achievement in learning and scholarship due to the contribution such works represent

[26] E.g., see Geiger, *Philosophy and the Social Order*, p. 144; see also theme of Dewey's *How We Think*.

in the progress of mankind, the experimentalist regards no knowledge as either sacrosanct or enduring.

It is also quite possible for a teacher to consider that he is teaching his students to think "scientifically" when he encourages them to speculate beyond what seems reasonable and verifiable in the world of sensory appearances. Such a teacher would be very much in tune with the highly creative and purely deductive method of reasoning employed by Albert Einstein in getting at knowledge about the nature of the universe—knowledge which typically defies what appears to be true to the human senses.

Einstein, for example, in arriving at his theory of relativity, did not go through the experimentalist's sequence of reflective thinking, nor did he test his findings in a controlled, laboratory situation against empirical data. He hit upon his fanciful theories through the highest form of creative and speculative thinking, his thought processes unfettered by convention and generally accepted ways of viewing the world and things in it.

When Einstein made his predictions concerning the variability of time and motion, he did not perform time-and-motion experiments within different physical systems scattered throughout the vastness of interstellar space. He reached his conclusions by an intricate series of abstract mathematical calculations. By the same token, his speculations about gravitational field and the spherical universe were described in terms of abstract mathematical equations, and they embodied scientific theories which sharply questioned the idea that the geometry of the universe must be the same as that revealed by the human senses here on the planet earth.[27] When Einstein formulated his principle on the equivalence of gravity and acceleration, he did not do this on the basis of experiments performed from a box actually suspended in space. He speculated what would be observed by a trained physicist if he were placed inside a windowless box somewhere in outer space and the box were accelerated and decelerated. Einstein's conclu-

[27] See descriptions of Einstein's creative approach to knowledge throughout Lincoln Barnett's *The Universe and Dr. Einstein*, 2nd rev. ed.

sion was that from the limited perspective of the physicist there would be no way of telling whether the observed behavior of objects in the box was due to gravitational pull exerted on the box by some massive body outside it or due to a steady acceleration of the box itself.[28]

The speculative dimension of modern scientific thought epitomized by Einstein ignores, in effect, the sensory limitations imposed by concepts of reality which insist that all things must be comprehensible to the human mind and free of paradox, ambiguity, and ultimate mystery. Moreover, speculative science has placed a premium on *intuitive* thinking—ideas that occur spontaneously, seemingly out of nowhere, instead of resulting from a systematic, analytic procedure.[29]

A teacher functioning from a speculative-intuitive intellectual framework might regard the experimentalist's concept of scientific method useful as far as it goes; however, he would consider rigid empirical delimitations as an intellectual strait jacket, and would encourage speculative inquiry on the part of his students as his highest educational aim. Rather than confining his students to definite progressive stages of learning, he would encourage them to make courageous leaps into the unknown:

> In contrast to analytic thinking, intuitive thinking characteristically does not advance in careful, well-defined steps. Indeed, it tends to involve maneuvers based seemingly on an implicit perception of the total problem. The thinker arrives at an answer, which may be right or wrong, with little if any awareness of the process by which he reached it. He rarely can provide an adequate account of how he obtained his answer, and he may be unaware of just what aspects of the problem situation he was responding to. Usually intuitive thinking rests on familiarity with the domain of knowledge in-

[28] George Gamow, *Matter, Earth, and Sky*, pp. 535–58.

[29] See Blythe Clinchy, "The Role of Intuition in Learning," *NEA Journal* (February, 1968), p. 33. See also John F. Wharton, "Does Anyone Know Reality?" pp. 21–23. Intuition, as an instrument of knowledge, is held to be a process in which truth is known by a flash of insight or immediate awareness—a discerning of understandings ahead of empirical evidence.

volved and with its structure, which makes it possible for the thinker to leap about, skipping steps and employing short cuts in a manner that requires a later rechecking of conclusions by more analytic means, whether deductive or inductive.[30]

Persons oriented to the philosophies of experimentalism and logical positivism[31] do use speculation and intuition as sources of hypotheses. However, neither philosophy equates speculative-intuitive inquiry with knowledge or truth. Whereas these processes are regarded as valued aspects of experience (in that they give rise to inspiration), they are *not* seen as valid replacements for the reflective method of inquiry or for analytic procedures which ultimately test truth empirically. This subordination of speculative-intuitive experience to empirical checks of knowledge is reflected in Jerome Bruner's statement reproduced above. Even realist philosophers who claim intuition of the mystical kind as a source of truth tend to put such knowledge to the test of nonintuitive methods before accepting it.[32]

In contrast, the philosophies of idealism and existentialism regard intuition as an indispensable and central means of knowing.[33] Both of these positions insist that there is no ground for accepting as correct *only* those insights used to support an empiricist theory of knowledge. In fact, among idealists and existentialists there is a certain scepticism about the presumed correctness of empirical data, an assumption

[30] Jerome Bruner, *The Process of Education* (Cambridge: Harvard University Press, 1960); paperback Vintage Books, 1960, p. 58.

[31] Logical positivism is discussed in Chapter 5, pp. 98–103; it is another empirically oriented system of belief.

[32] Cf. J. Donald Butler, *Four Philosophies and Their Practice in Education and Religion*, p. 284. A notable exception would be religious realism—Thomism, or Neo-Scholasticism, which holds that a spiritual "intuition of first principles" is a superior kind of knowledge. See, e.g., Jacques Maritain, "Thomist Views on Education," in *Modern Philosophies and Education*, ed. Nelson B. Henry, pp. 58, 60.

[33] Cf. Butler, *Four Philosophies*, p. 237; and Robert G. Olson, "The Human Condition," in *Modern Movements in Educational Philosophy*, ed. Van Cleve Morris, pp. 310–13.

which is deeply embedded in experimentalist, logical positivist, and realist philosophies. This scepticism of empirical knowledge by idealists and existentialists has an interesting affinity with the outlook of non-Newtonian speculative science. Einstein, for example, was quite willing to forego the possibility of rechecking many of his conclusions empirically. Is it not possible, he asked, that man is being deceived in his desire to want to picture everything in the universe according to the data he receives from his limited senses? Is it not possible, he also asked, that man has a habit of holding to unwarranted assumptions about the *structure* of reality itself—assumptions derived from the way things *seem* to be? For example, might not man's perception of his immediate world, with its "obvious" Euclidean basis, encourage him to project a distorted view when it comes to the totality of reality?

We confidently assume, for example, that two parallel beams of light will travel through space forever without meeting, because in the infinite plane of Euclidean geometry parallel lines never meet. We also feel certain that in outer space, as on a tennis court, a straight line is the shortest distance between two points. And yet Euclid never actually *proved* that a straight line is the shortest distance between two points; he simply arbitrarily *defined* a straight line as the shortest distance between two points.[34]

The paradox, ambiguity, and ultimate mystery associated with modern speculative science—and the resulting implications for the human mind which seems so obsessed with "common sense" empirical data—also have been expressed by James Conant, a chemist by profession:

The idea that there could be two diametrically opposed theories as to the nature of heat, of light, or of matter, and that both could be rejected and confirmed as a consequence of experiments would have been considered nonsense to almost all sane people fifty years ago.

[34] Lincoln Barnett, *The Universe and Dr. Einstein*, 2nd rev. ed. (New York: Mentor Books, 1957), p. 94. Copyright, 1957, by Lincoln Barnett. Reprinted by permission of William Morrow & Company, Inc., Publishers.

... In regard to light, we can hardly do better than say that light is in a sense both undulatory and corpuscular. In regard to matter, we have already seen that here too a certain ambiguity has entered in . . . the physicist has learned to live with a paradox that once seemed intolerable. It might be better to say that he has discovered how general is the paradox and by what mathematical manipulations of experimental data he can get forward with all manner of undertakings because of the paradox.[35]

Conant followed with a quotation from P. W. Bridgman:

Finally, I come to what it seems to me may well be from the long range point of view the most revolutionary of the insights to be derived from our recent experiences in physics, more revolutionary than the insights afforded by the discoveries of Galileo and Newton, or of Darwin. This is the insight that *it is impossible to transcend the human reference point.* . . . The new insight comes from a realization that the structure of nature may eventually be such that our processes of thought do not correspond to it sufficiently to permit us to think about it at all. We have already had an intimation of this in the behavior of very small things in the quantum domain . . . there can be no difference of opinion with regard to the dilemma that now confronts us in the direction of the very small. *We are now approaching a bound beyond which we are forever stopped from pushing our inquiries, not by the construction of the world, but by the construction of ourselves.* . . . We are confronted with something truly ineffable. We have reached the limit of the vision of the great pioneers of science, the vision, namely, that we live in a sympathetic world, in that it is comprehensible by our minds. [Italics added.][36]

[35] James B. Conant, *Modern Science and Modern Man* (New York: Columbia University Press, 1952), pp. 41, 47.

[36] P. W. Bridgman, "Philosophical Implications of Physics," in *The American Academy of Arts and Science Bulletin* (February, 1950), p. 5. Cf. Werner Heisenberg, *The Physicist's Conception of Nature*, trans. Arnold J. Pomerans. It should be noted here that there are significant differences between Einstein's *theory of relativity* and the *quantum theory* developed by Planck, Heisenberg, and others. However, both theories are identified with modern speculative science, and they do support each other in their radical departure from classical empirical science.

A teacher functioning against the backdrop of speculative-intuitive science would take care not to discourage unique approaches to learning. Rather than demanding immediate and justifiable proof for every new idea which surfaces, such a teacher would encourage his students to nourish and develop their embryonic ideas with the same freedom that enables an artist to give birth to a painting. Also, he would help his students *accept errors and the whole phenomenon of making mistakes as a necessary and valuable aspect of learning,* not as something to be avoided or penalized. In fostering an atmosphere in which students feel free to formulate new ways of looking at things and doing things—whether writing an essay, interpreting world history, fashioning a wooden book-end, solving a mathematical problem, or painting a portrait—such a teacher would be most reluctant to impose formulas or patterns as standards against which potentially new forms of excellence must be judged. He would realize that whereas the opinions of experts might be valuable in giving impetus to new thought, an educational premium on "the accumulated wisdom of mankind" might stultify creative genius.

Now in the light of the foregoing discussion, what does it actually mean to develop the rational powers and to think logically and scientifically? It can be seen that an operational definition of rationality involves an *a priori* value judgment representing whatever position the individual chooses to hold and whatever kind of authority he regards as final—whatever the degree of finality or tentativeness he attaches to the authority.

Frequently a sharp distinction is made between *a priori* thinking, in which knowledge is derived from and validated by transempirical forms of reason, and *a posteriori* thinking, in which knowledge is derived from and validated either wholly or in part by sensory experience. In the "show me" atmosphere of a heavily materialistic culture, *a posteriori* knowledge is likely to enjoy much greater credibility. However, what needs to be understood by the educator is that even if a person chooses to regard empirical data as the most valid test of truth, *his decision not to transcend sensory experience required an initial* a priori *value judgment*. In effect, we all start from ground zero in our belief systems. Whatever the concept of reality, it involves an act of faith on the part of the believer. This is as true of the laboratory technician convinced of the basic reality of his sensory data as it is of the mystic convinced of the fundamental reality of his nonsensory experiences. Consequently *all* basic assumptions about the nature of reality, man, knowledge, values, and how man learns lie beyond the empirical test of verifiable, sharable proof.

Obviously no one meaning of rationality can be arrived at which will satisfy all persons. Therefore, the attempt of teachers to use the development-of-rational-powers directive as a guide in planning and carrying out classroom activities is bound to lead to diverse and confusing interpretations.[37] Evaluation of the success or failure of students in achieving the desired goal of rationality likewise is bound to be based on diverse and confusing criteria. Since students are moved into, around, up, and out of the American school system on the basis of the kinds of criteria which educators establish for evaluating performance, the multiplicity of meanings of this proposed goal of rationality is of no small consequence.

For the classroom teacher, who is where the action is and who must plan and organize learning activities in a concrete way, what alternative is there to consensus, to the resolution of these very real differences in our basic philosophies of life and in our resulting educational philosophies? It is conceivable, of course, that experts could formulate more definitive educational goals and values, establishing operational-level objectives which would be binding upon all teachers and all students. These experts could replace our present foundational-level quagmire with firm ground, providing us with an unequivocal set of guidelines. However, such a course would

[37] Cf. Theodore Brameld, "What Is the Central Purpose of American Education?" in *Crucial Issues in the Teaching of Social Studies*, ed. Byron G. Massialas and Andreas M. Kazamias, pp. 14–19.

be at the expense of cultural pluralism. Furthermore, a serious problem would be posed in the designation of the experts who would carry out a sweeping program of this sort. Just *who* would they be?

It is also conceivable that in the continuing absence of a clear-cut national consensus at the operational level, teachers could simply dispense with goals and values as they plan their classroom experiences. Since relatively few teachers actually work through a consciously recognized philosophy, it might be argued that this approach already has been opted. If so, such a practice is reminiscent of the moron looking for a village somewhere. Picked up by a driver and given a lift, he was asked if he could read the highway sign. He replied, "Yep, I can read some of it. I can read how fur, but I can't read where to."[38]

I believe that a more viable alternative does exist, and I have set it forth in the following chapter. However, the reader should be advised that my proposed alternative is firmly rooted in two basic assumptions, both of which share an attribute of all basic assumptions: they lie beyond empirical verification.

My first assumption is that *cultural pluralism is the most important value in the American ideological core.* This value, it seems to me, is primary since it sustains the right to life of all other values. Although pluralism may present us with an intellectual quagmire of sorts, I am satisfied that its potential strengths—like that of hybrid vigor—more than offset the difficulties.

My second assumption is that *controversy is the very life-blood of a democratic society* and therefore is a healthy, necessary dimension of its educational system. Without controversy, cultural pluralism becomes a myth!

[38] As quoted in Calvin Grieder and Stephen Romine, *American Education*, 3d ed. (New York: The Ronald Press Company, © 1965), p. 146.

CHAPTER FOUR

A WHOLISTIC APPROACH

A teacher will be frustrated—both during his professional preparation and throughout his teaching career—unless he faces up to the full implications of what it is to live and teach in a society which thus far has permitted the expression of very diverse beliefs and values. Since there is no generally accepted "right" way to think about much of anything, matters of foundational conflict must be resolved (if they are to be resolved) at the level of the individual's own basic assumptions—that is, at the level of his personal core beliefs. The teacher must be willing to assume responsibility for working out *his own answers* to many of the problems he will encounter in the classroom regarding goals and values and how to implement them. Instead of looking outside himself for direction, the individual teacher needs to begin his professional life with a profoundly searching interior look at *himself*. In short, the most important aspect of professional preparation is an on-going critical examination of all ideas and suggestions against a total philosophic frame of reference which has deep meaning for a person in terms of its application to his full life.

This critical examination of ideas should be, of course, a continuing process throughout the teacher's professional life. As his experience and knowledge expand, he needs consciously to integrate such knowledge into his central core of beliefs. In the process, the individual usually finds that his philosophic outlook undergoes constant reevaluation and growth.

What should be clear at this juncture is that there should be no separation between a teacher's total philosophy of life, his philosophy of education, his learning theory, and his methodology. In other words, his methodology, learning theory, and educational philosophy should be conscious derivatives of the basic assumptions he holds regarding the nature of the world, knowledge, and values—or, in more conventional philosophic terms, his metaphysical, epistemological, and axiological beliefs.[1]

THE PHILOSOPHY-METHODOLOGY PYRAMID

This intimate relationship might be illustrated by a pyramid, with the base representing a teacher's total philosophy of life. Just as there should be a horizontal line of consistency running through the tripartite structure of the base philosophy itself—that is, through the world, knowledge, and value views —a vertical line of consistency should run through the derivative educational philosophy, learning theory, and the visible result of the whole theoretical structure: the teaching methodology.

That is to say, a teacher should at all times be able to justify his methodology in terms of his philosophy. Let us assume, for example, that a teacher regards the temporal world of physical reality as the starting point of a belief system, and that the things in the natural world are real, independent facts which have an existence separate from man himself. Suppose

[1] The world-view (metaphysics), knowledge-view (epistemology), and value-view (axiology) form the three components of any fully developed philosophic system.

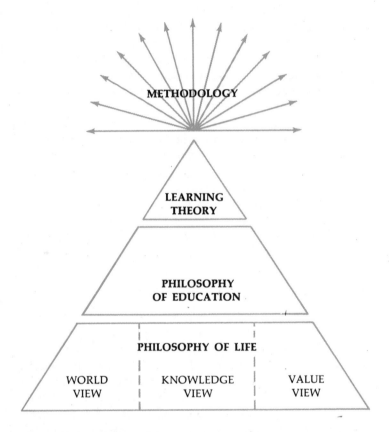

Illustration A *Philosophy-Methodology "Pyramid"*

he further believes that the world of nature is an orderly, accurate, and objective world wherein no single event happens by chance—that all things in the universe operate according to a law of cause and effect. Therefore, when something occurs, he regards it as the only thing that could have taken place. Following this line of reasoning, the teacher would be quite consistent if he views man as a being who has a constant nature, who functions within the cosmic law of cause and effect, and who acts in the only way he can act in relation to the surrounding environment in which he finds himself.

Against the above *world-view* beliefs, the teacher might hold the compatible *knowledge-view* that all knowledge comes to us by way of sensory experience, that the mind is similar to a blank sheet of paper which records impressions that are made thereon, and that the human mind is passive as it experiences the natural world.

If he is to be consistent, the teacher will then build his *value-view* on assumptions compatible with the rest of his basic philosophy. For example, he might hold that values also have an independent existence from man and are to be found in the structure of nature itself. From this position, the teacher is likely to hold that "good" is all of those things which adjust man to his environment and "evil" is that which estranges him. Since the teacher regards human nature as constant and unchanging, he probably will consider values that adjust the individual to his society to be the enduring values of mankind.

If the teacher proceeds to build his *philosophy of education* upon his core beliefs, it is quite possible that he will see his role as that of an adjusting agent between the student and the enduring values and ideas which embody the good life. In other words, he will have the general aim of codifying the good life, the good individual, and the good society, and he will then attempt to translate these ideals into particular learnings which he thinks will help students realize these ideals. Specifically, he will see himself as one who exercises authority over his students to instruct them in knowledge, skills, attitudes, and values which he deems necessary if they are to recognize their true nature and the highest good.

Should the teacher then extend his thinking to *learning theory,* he will need to consider it against his assumption that students are passive receptors of external stimuli. Since he believes that people behave in terms of the environmental factors to which they are exposed, it is possible that he will regard subject matter, per se, as the focal point of learning.

Therefore, he probably will arrange and manipulate the subject matter in a way designed to lead his students toward the desired understandings. Because the teacher sees students as creatures who respond in terms of cause-and-effect relationships, he also is likely to place a heavy emphasis on extrinsic motivation—on incentives to evoke intended learnings.

At the practical level of operation, the teacher might employ an array of *methods*. For example, he might lecture extensively, have students memorize quantities of data, have them engage in simulation games, oral reports, group discussions, and question-and-answer sessions. He might utilize programmed materials. He might cultivate a friendship with his students and thereby encourage imitation of the desired kinds of behavior which he exemplifies. But if he projects his theoretical structure into actual classroom practice, whatever methodology he employs with his students will be in effect a "pouring in" of the external information and ideas which should be known. The extrinsic motivation might take the form of test scores and other visible signs of student achievement. He might find that a simple shake of his head or a "Yes, that's correct!" will suffice to indicate to his students that they are on the proper learning track.

Although the cluster of metaphysical assumptions in the above illustration could give rise to a very different pyramid, nonetheless it can be seen that the structure built from the initial premise of the mythical teacher represents a consistent, coherent whole. And whether or not one is in agreement with this particular whole, it must be said that within the stated system of beliefs the covert rationale for the teaching methodology and the resulting overt actions are reasonable and comprehensible.

Although scholars have tended to cluster certain kinds of basic assumptions into various philosophic systems of thought, probably few persons identify themselves as pure exponents of any one system.[2] This philosophic eclecticism

[2] There is no agreement on the number of philosophic systems of thought in existence. Typically scholars discuss various forms of idealism, realism, and experimentalism (pragmatism); also some of the newer

might encourage some individuals to entertain an inconsistent and incoherent collection of assumptions—a phenomenon which gives rise to much confusion in the upper regions of the proposed pyramid. But eclecticism can provide other individuals with the freedom to build a philosophy of life that is open to far-ranging and personally enriching ideas:

The eclectic view does not necessarily imply accepting all opposing philosophic and psychological positions, for this may lead to accepting diametrically opposed views that cancel each other and leave the would-be eclectic with nothing to hold onto save conflicting and confusing ideas. A distinction should be made here between the eclecticism based on the formulation of a point of view by addition of a number of conflicting views and that based on making one's outlook large enough to incorporate the good elements of other philosophic and psychological positions without damaging one's own central position. Just as in political parties we have narrowly defined positions or liberal positions regardless of the label we may attach to the party, so also in philosophic positions we may have provincialism or universalism of outlook. One may be a narrow realist, rationalist, or idealist to the complete exclusion of whatever may be worthwhile in other positions, or one may be liberal enough to hold to the core of a given position but widen the circle of belief to allow for inclusion of ideas from other camps without damaging one's identification with that central position.[3]

---

schools like existentialism, logical positivism, and language analysis. For example, see George F. Kneller, *Introduction to the Philosophy of Education*; also J. Donald Butler, *Four Philosophies and Their Practice in Education and Religion*, 3rd ed. However, Philip H. Phenix considered thirteen philosophies representative of "the main varieties of positions" in American education; see his *Philosophies of Education*. The National Society for the Study of Education considered nine essays as representing "the tenets of major schools of thought" in contemporary American philosophy; see *Modern Philosophies and Education*, ed. Nelson B. Henry. The profusion of educational philosophies is a result of the fact that a particular metaphysical core of beliefs gives rise to numerous interpretations.

[3] Mehdi Nakosteen, *The History and Philosophy of Education* (New York: The Ronald Press Company, © 1965), p. 566.

It is important to recognize that the schema of thinking described in this chapter can be held by the individual as a static set of ideas—much like the outlook of the pharaohs, whose stone pyramids were built to endure for all time. Given such an outlook, the teacher is likely to reject any concept of change and to view his own pyramid—and his derivative methodology—as similarly static. One can only remind such a teacher of Shelley's poem "Ozymandias," inspired by an inscription on an ancient Egyptian monument:

> "My name is Ozymandias, king of kings;
> Look on my works, ye Mighty, and despair!"
> Nothing beside remains. Round the decay
> Of that colossal wreck, boundless and bare
> The lone and level sands stretch far away.[4]

NEUTRALITY AND OBJECTIVITY

The idea that there should be a close relationship between a teacher's philosophy and his methodology does not mean I believe he should try to indoctrinate his students with that philosophy. The point I am making here is that a neutral teacher—one who doesn't commit himself to anything for fear of offending someone—simply is not effective in the classroom.

The issue of indoctrination can be clarified by differentiating between two oft-confused terms: neutrality and objectivity. Neutrality is an attitude of intellectual and emotional blandness; when reflected by a teacher, it tends to elicit a similar response in his students. Objectivity (at least insofar as I am comfortable in using the term) refers to the quality of intellectual integrity in viewing all knowledge. It can be argued that objectivity can only be approximated at best, since a teacher's perception and understanding of the world in which he lives are deeply influenced by his own life experiences and belief system. Nonetheless, *relative objectivity* can be attained through a persistent, conscientious effort to

[4] Percy Bysshe Shelley, "Ozymandias."

approach all phenomena with the attitude of open, critical inquiry. Phrased another way, bias is not a negative factor in teaching; quite to the contrary, it is part of the human condition to function as an evaluating creature. One simply cannot think about anything with a degree of serious attention *without developing a point of view.* An individual who claims to be without bias in any matter of consequence is in effect a non-thinker.

It is precisely this human habit of forming points of view which needs to be openly recognized and then carefully examined in relation to one's own core level of beliefs and the core beliefs held by others. A teacher who regards objectivity and bias in this light is likely to accord the same opportunities for open recognition and careful examination to his students. He also is more likely to gear his teaching toward deliberately provoking different opinions among his students. He will realize that only in a classroom which serves as an arena for the sharing of conflicting ideas and interpretations can he reasonably expect to encourage the development of points of view among his students instead of parrotlike thinking and behaving. Indoctrination, or the deliberate imposition of ideas in such a learning atmosphere, would be an antithetical process.

THE TURNED-ON TEACHER

The above comments about bias, objectivity, and a distinctive point of view have direct bearing on the entire teaching personality. Since 1964, I have had extensive opportunity to observe secondary teaching situations. These observations, coupled with my earlier impressions as a high school teacher, have convinced me that the educator who turns students on is all too rare. Sidney Jourard's description[5] of the stultification and stupefaction which is fostered in many classrooms is well founded. I am convinced, too, that this matter of turning students on doesn't lend itself to a prescribed formula,

[5] Sidney M. Jourard, "The Human Challenge of Automation," *Disclosing Man to Himself,* pp. 187–99.

nor does it readily lend itself to the remoteness of textbook advice. Yet those all-too-rare learning situations which are alive with excitement and mutual involvement do seem to reflect certain teaching qualities. *Empathy* may be the most appropriate term to describe the feeling tone established in these classrooms. Such teachers convey a deep respect for their students. They regard them as infinitely varied and remarkable beings, not as objects to be manipulated.

Most significantly, turned-on teachers tend to radiate a wholeness as they approach their students; for them living and teaching seem to be two aspects of the same process. They are free of "tunnel vision"—that circumscribed approach to a subject which looks out on a highly limited segment of life. Instead, the turned-on teacher invariably sees his field of specialized knowledge as a focal point for getting at a much larger world. He encourages his students, too, to break through the artificial walls of the discipline. In the hands of such a teacher, the subject-matter content is never treated in a mundane, matter-of-fact way. Whether an analysis of an amoeba in a biology class, an atom in a physics class, a sonnet in an English class, quadratic equations in an algebra class, or the Four River Valley Civilizations in a social studies class, the topic at hand is ultimately related to the larger questions of human life—the speculative how and why. In short, these teachers are quite philosophic in their handling of subject-matter content. And since the big philosophic questions are relevant to all of us—simply because we are human beings who must live and die, and who must cope with an immense range of joys, sorrows, problems, and pleasures—the truly turned-on teacher who sees a profound philosophic relevancy in his field of inquiry is able to communicate this sense of relevancy to his students.

Since so much of the dissatisfaction and disillusionment among American students is couched in cries of educational irrelevancy, the motivation of the turned-on teacher cannot be minimized. Curriculum content is bound to appear irrelevant to students when teachers themselves have not worked through the philosophic significance of their own specialties of knowledge. Minutiae thereby become all-important; both teachers and students get bogged down with trivial details, the possession of which seldom affects the direction of any-one's life. Teachers so occupied, if pressed for reasons why they are taking a group of students through a study of history, grammar, literature, foreign language, or mathematics, are likely to respond, "Well, they need to know it!" And to queries of "Why?" they will insist: "It's in the textbook!" or "The curriculum is set up this way, and it's expected that we cover this!" or "If they don't know this, they won't be able to pass the district-wide standardized test at the end of the year!" or "If they don't know this, they won't be able to go on to the next grade!" or "They have to know this to get into college!" These reasons, although commonly voiced, are bogus ones in the business of real learning. Knowledge has no genuine meaning for any individual, whatever the subject, unless he can see the connection between that knowl-edge and the totality of his life.

MULTIPLE-BELIEF SYSTEMS

All the above considerations lead me to believe that in the final analysis it really doesn't matter *what* philosophy a teacher chooses to hold. What *does* matter is that he formu-late a foundation for his thinking and that he project this intellectual orientation to his students. I am suggesting here that teaching effectiveness cannot be correlated with any one cluster of basic assumptions about the good, the true, and the beautiful—nor with any one derivative set of beliefs about the way in which students can and should learn. Indeed, I welcome the educational implications that would accompany the recognized existence of different belief systems among teachers—namely, the exposing of students to the widest pos-sible range of alternatives. With the exposure of students to a multiplicity of fundamental ideas and values, the chances would be high that no one teacher would be successful in blatantly indoctrinating students to his view.

I do not wish to recommend the "widest possible range of

alternatives" in an absolute sense. For example, I would not condone deliberate exposure of students to teachers who possess sets of core beliefs which cause them to negate the worth and capabilities of their students and/or which lead them to treat students in an intolerant, brutal, and inhuman manner. However, there is no single set of core beliefs which corners the market in respecting students as worthy, able human beings. Also, there is no single cluster of assumptions which corners the market in deeply caring about the well-being of students. Furthermore, it is only through thought-provoking exposure to the spectrum of human beliefs and values that a student will be stimulated to fashion a system of beliefs which *he* can hold with the conviction of personally derived meaning. Such exposure is also likely to enhance the student's understanding and appreciation of alternatives, re-gardless of the belief system which he chooses for himself. It seems to me that the oft-stated ideals of individual freedom and cultural pluralism can be achieved in no other way.

I do not wish to convey here a sanction of the idea that one philosophy is just as good as any other. This belief, often suggested as the most democratic and desirable attitude, seems to me the height of naïveté. On what basis could an individual possibly hold something to be good and true, use that something to provide concrete guidelines for his life and all the decisions he must make, and at the same time pretend that he might just as well be operating from some other philosophic basis? Such a mentality might, indeed, exhibit flexibility and a convenient expediency of behavior—like the reed which bends with each new wind. However, it would scarcely lend itself to the development of personal *convictions* —beliefs which stem from careful selection and on-going eval-uation. In short, what the individual says he holds as truth (however tentative) ought to be regarded by him as the best of truths; else he has no legitimate reason for espousing his brand of truth in the first place. This posture need not, of course, deter him from appreciating, respecting, and sustain-ing the right to existence of very different convictions about the good, the true, and the beautiful—regarding life in general and teaching in particular.

I am mindful that in the quest for social order and harmony many persons constantly look for the *one* best alternative in all matters of any consequence—whether the issue is that of ascertaining the most desirable teaching style or how human lives in general should be lived. In my opinion, this quest is inevitably narcissistic and, as such, undermines both an individual's right to his own unique humanness and our national commitment to pluralism. But I am equally mindful of the many other contemporary voices which, in the very names of individualism and cultural pluralism, deny that there is any possible intersection of values which can serve as a basis for social cohesion and social movement. These latter thinkers invariably follow the line of reasoning that since there is no single body of truth which enjoys universal acceptance, there is little point in searching for a common social ethic. They argue that, instead, all persons should be encouraged to do their own thing. It appears to me that this latter position undermines cultural pluralism no less than promoting one "best" way of life. Doing one's own thing all too often carries with it a sense of responsibility to no one except oneself; that is, it encourages an egocentric orientation, which is bound to create a breach between the individual and others—a breach born of callous insensitivity to the feelings, values, and beliefs of one's fellowmen.

I believe that the "I-Thou" relationship, so eloquently expressed by Martin Buber,[6] suggests a viable basis for sustaining both individual freedom and the well-being and continuity of the larger social group: it requires that the individual work through his personal meanings and values first so that he is comfortable and secure enough to be *capable* of reaching out and extending himself in authentic relationships with other people. Such an individual, as deeply committed to the well-being of others as he is to himself, is more likely

[6] Martin Buber, *I and Thou.*

to search for points of *accommodation* with his fellows, rather than to approach them with an attitude of disdain, persuasion, or conversion. In this latter instance, areas for common policy-making and/or action can be sought wherever possible, but the reasons undergirding each individual's thinking are regarded as inviolate.

By way of illustration: Two very different teachers might well accommodate their viewpoints when it comes to the issue of the kinds of students they want to have in their classes. The one, holding to a deeply theistic rooting of values (and appealing perhaps to what he believes to be a divinely ordained fraternal ethic), could nonetheless find agreement with his agnostic but deeply humanistic colleague (who might hold to values rooted in empirical data abstracted from the social sciences) that school policy and practice should include racial integration. These two teachers certainly could work with one another at the level of action for the achievement of such a policy; however, *the different sanctions which motivate them toward a similar social goal could continue to be respected.*

Admittedly, such accommodation cannot be achieved in all matters of life, and certainly not in all matters pertaining to education. Yet accommodation wherever possible—whether between professional educators, between educators and the lay community, or between teachers and their students—is infinitely preferable in my opinion to the alternative of ignoring the significance of each individual's foundational beliefs or of searching for a uniform mode of life, of learning, and of teaching.

No doubt some readers will find my subjectivity about multiple-belief systems disconcerting and will conjure up visions of social chaos and the emergence of Hitler types. This prospect is not, of course, what I have in mind. What I am pointing out is that *to insist that persons function according to identical, prescribed criteria within any of our social institutions, including our schools, invariably discourages pluralism.* I associate pluralism with an open society, and hold that no society can be fully open which negates alternative ways of thinking and behaving, and has only "one avenue of approved entry into the mainstream of dignity."[7] In response to possible nervousness on the part of the reader in the face of deliberately vague social rules and regulations, I would point out that a truly open, pluralistic society is critically dependent upon a knowledgeable citizenry actively involved in working out the direction of their lives. By a knowledgeable citizenry, I mean people who are educated to have more than a superficial acquaintance with the world in which they live—people who know something about mankind's rich social, intellectual, and esthetic heritage. Such citizens would have a basis for bringing *perspective* to what was, what is, and what might be. By actively involved, I mean the opposite of passive acquiescers—those socially apathetic souls upon whom a Hitler mentality feeds. Active involvement implies a habit of dialoguing with one another in all the vital matters of group living, and at levels much deeper than innocuous platitudes. Dialogue is not recommended simply because it might be interesting to discover that we human beings do not think alike. On-going dialogue enables us to give serious thought to the present and long-range consequences of our behavior toward one another in all the affairs of community living, and to seek points of accommodation.

Implicit in the above suggestion is the idea that our social institutions—again, including our schools—should be regarded not as coercive organs of social control but as central clearinghouses of information which operate on the basis of a broad decentralization of authority. To be sure, I am not ignoring the need for policy development and decision-making. I am suggesting that these are functions which are not dependent upon monistic organs of social control but can be sought after in the give-and-take interaction of loosely organized human beings. And I am referring here to *authentic interaction,* in which mutual respect and ideological differences are not viewed in an antithetical sense.

Paul Goodman has written beautifully about this clearing-

7 Cf. Peter Schrag, "End of the Impossible Dream," p. 68.

house concept of social institutions, in which criteria for decision-making ultimately reside with individuals in specific situations.[8] Goodman describes his ideas as those of a "Jeffersonian anarchist." The phrase has merit. In any event, I see neither his position nor mine as sanctioning the disastrous social upheavals typically associated with anarchist thinking. Like Goodman, I believe that conflict which surfaces in a society in which authority is highly decentralized actually is *a stabilizing phenomenon*. The clearinghouse idea is predicated on a deep faith in human potential, and a belief in the social bonds which can be established between persons who have *a basic trust in one another*. It is an idea in human relationships that as yet remains untried on a large scale, even in our own much-heralded "free, open, and pluralistic" society.

THE TEACHER AS A WHOLE PERSON

Each of us, I imagine, has his own private list of good teachers—those men and women who seared our minds forever. If we would recall the educational aims and teaching methods of those great educators, we undoubtedly would find a heterogeneous assortment of ideas and practices. My own list includes a teacher who might be described as a classical realist—a woman who took a group of teen-agers through Shakespearean drama, had them absorb lengthy passages, and led them toward a permanent appreciation of the poet's style and scope of thinking. And all of this she pursued as a great labor of love. My list also includes an experimentalist psychology teacher—a man who conveyed an almost missionary zeal for improving the quality of life here on the planet earth.

These two teachers, along with the others on my list, never lost sight of the forest for the trees. Whatever the particular learning task at hand, none of them became preoccupied with form to the neglect of important ideas and values. In retrospect, the only real thread of commonality I can find among

[8] Paul Goodman, *New Reformation: Notes of a Neolithic Conservative*, pp. 12–20.

them all is that each one came through to me as a *whole person*, and each one somehow aroused a recognition of the need for wholeness in my own life.

Having designated the point of origin of the development of a professional teacher as the formation of a deeply meaningful, wholistic philosophy, I further recommend that *the individual teacher's personal point of view be regarded as the best key to selection and development of curriculum content in the classroom situation*. This is not to suggest that the content of a particular course should not be part of an overall school curriculum planned through staff collaboration. It is also not to defy the no-man-is-an-island factor in human life. However, it does assume that in any given set of circumstances the individual teacher can choose his attitude—his own way. It also assumes that within the given set of circumstances a wide latitude of freedom for choosing does exist for him,[9] and that along with that freedom, there also exists personal responsibility for his actions.

Classroom teachers frequently complain that they are unable to exercise much independent judgment within the bureaucratic structure of the modern school. But the real issue, I would like to point out, is whether a professional educator is willing to assume full responsibility for the consequences of whatever decisions he *does* make. Many teachers who could influence educational developments find it more expedient to rationalize their helplessness in terms of power-structure myths. Interestingly enough, the bureaucratic nature of our contemporary social institutions actually helps to sustain a considerable latitude of freedom, more than appears on the surface. Bureaucracies, whether in business or in education, tend to flourish in an atmosphere of diffused responsibility, wherein a nebulous, corporate decision-making prevails in most matters and buck-passing reigns as a highly developed art. Although an individual, indeed, risks censure for personal initiative and boat-rocking in any bureaucratic

[9] Cf. Viktor E. Frankl, *Man's Search for Meaning*, p. 104; Rollo May, *Love and Will*, pp. 196–204; and Charles Suhor, "The Bogey Man . . . Search and Destroy," pp. 78, 75.

framework, the freedom to assume such a risk nonetheless is always present.

Once the very broad nature and goals of a course of study have been established and some general topics or areas have been recommended by the full teaching staff, it should be up to the individual teacher to flesh out those sketchy curriculum guides into specific course content and purposes. And since the potential data in any field of study are infinite, the selection of specific content should be made by the teacher in terms of what he deems significant *as viewed from his total philosophic frame of reference*. Such content should reflect his own unique sense of relevancy and consequently would be the kind of data around which he can best generate a sense of excitement and relevancy to his students.

As the teacher approaches his particular curriculum specialty, he necessarily will assume the role of *both* a generalist and a specialist since he brings a total world-view perspective to the situation. For example, if history is the special focal point of a teacher, that specialty will pose no curriculum boundaries for him. He will draw to the study of history whatever data in the full range of human activities he views as important. The possible domain of interests for a history teacher functioning from such a perspective is shown in *Illustration B*.

The extent of the teacher's involvement in all fields of knowledge will, of course, be intimately related to the dimensions of his own vision. For any teacher to assume the demanding role of both specialist and generalist might appear presumptuous and impossible. However, I would submit that such a role *is* possible *if the teacher also regards himself as a student who is thoroughly caught up in a lifelong process of expanding his own knowledge.*

It seems to me that a teacher can regard his particular point of view in one of two broad ways: He can regard it as the desired vision not only for himself but for all the lives he touches in his capacity as a teacher. Or he can regard it as his own profoundly personal source of meaning and direction —and use it more as an activating force in creating a wholistic

PHILOSOPHY

PSYCHOLOGY   POLITICAL SCIENCE

LANGUAGES   ANTHROPOLOGY

SCIENCE   GEOGRAPHY

HISTORY

MUSIC   ECONOMICS

ART   RELIGION

SOCIOLOGY   LITERATURE

INTERNATIONAL RELATIONS

Illustration B   *A world-view perspective of the history curriculum*

approach to life among his students. In an increasingly inter-dependent world, in which the well-being of each of us at every moment hinges upon mutual understanding, trust, and respect among persons of diverse thought, I am convinced that the latter way is the better one. It gives full expression to the teacher's uniqueness but at the same time encourages and sustains uniqueness among his students.

The significance of a wholistic teaching vision—one which extends to the world beyond the classroom—can be illustrated by a curriculum case in point. The teaching of art in the American secondary school does not enjoy a particularly high status in contrast with the "hard-core, essential" academic subjects. By many, art courses are regarded as frills—as a pleasant, leisure-time pursuit of youthful dilettantes. Some art teachers, seeking to bolster the status of their work, employ rigorous standards of performance wherein excellence is determined on the basis of the student's ability to reproduce the classic shadow-box-with-the-iris or other teacher models of how reality should look. But there is another view of the role of art in the school curriculum, a view which goes far beyond frills and replication of shadow-box objects. Such a view was described by John Dewey in his 1934 book, *Art as Experience:*

The sense of increase of understanding, of a deepened intelligibility on the part of objects of nature and man, resulting from esthetic experience, has led philosophic theorists to treat art as a mode of knowledge, and has induced artists, especially poets, to regard art as a mode of revelation of the inner nature of things that cannot be had in any other way. . . . What is intimated to my mind, is, that in both production and enjoyed perception of works of art, knowledge is transformed; it becomes something more than knowledge because it is merged with non-intellectual elements to form an experience worth while as an experience. . . . Tangled scenes of life are made more intelligible in esthetic experience.[10]

During my own junior and senior high school experiences as a student, it was my privilege to study with an art teacher who conveyed Dewey's vision of esthetic experience. In retrospect, it is difficult to imagine that any students could have passed through Edna Denniston's classes without being deeply affected by contact with this rare woman. She was, first of all, a highly talented, creative artist in her own right and a master technician in the skills of watercolor painting, oils, charcoal, pen-and-ink sketching, and in the knowledges of anatomy, perspective, drafting, printing, and shadow rendition. However, Denny's classes included much more than learning how to sketch on rice paper. Such activities served as the immediate task, but they were only springboards to a much larger world of experience. Her personality was not overwhelming; yet she radiated a quiet, penetrating force that somehow communicated her universal interests and concerns. It was her custom, for example, to print brief passages from

[10] John Dewey, *Art as Experience* (New York: Minton, Balch & Company, 1934), pp. 288, 290.

Kahlil Gibran's *The Prophet* on the chalkboard in the front of her room. Such passages appeared each day without comment; they were simply there. Exposure to this Lebanese philosopher-poet remains one of the most significant learning experiences of those years.

Since our high school on Long Island was only an hour's journey from some of the great art masterpieces of the world, Denny sponsored countless field trips to New York City. Although in later years I lived and worked in Manhattan and saw much of the ugliness of that metropolis, New York has remained for me a marvelous kaleidoscope of art galleries, museums, and monumental works of man. Under Denny's guidance, the city revealed its warmth, color, excitement—and most of all its humanity. There was always something to see beyond the immediacy of the canvasses in the Museum of Modern Art. The thick, palette-knife strokes of Vincent Van Gogh served as a door through which I glimpsed the life of one sensitive, moving human being. And Denny's introduction to Peter Blume's "The Eternal City" with its acid-green, jack-in-the-box head of Mussolini made a deeper impact on me than all the dry accounts of fascism in my social studies textbooks. As we would tour the streets of Greenwich Village, where each spring hundreds of artists hold their sidewalk displays, there was always much to see and to feel beyond the immediacy of that Bohemian world.

In essence, this art educator's whole approach to teaching was motivated by the desire to encourage an esthetic sensitivity in her students to everything they experienced. This she was able to do because she herself radiated a broad awareness and sensitivity. In a technologically oriented culture, in which expediency rather than taste governs the thinking and outlook of so many of us, the vision of arousing a sense of beauty in others is a grand vision indeed. And at a time when instant communication is bombarding us with reminders of the grotesque dimension of the twentieth century, I remain inspired by Edna Denniston's shared vision of so many years ago—a vision that sought always to find in the world of everyday affairs the equally real dimension of beauty.

In the event that the relationship between the world-view of the teacher and that of the student is not yet clearly perceived, let me suggest the following: In a technological society, where specialized knowledge and skill often serve as the dominant educational focal points, the world-view that is subtly promoted to the young tends increasingly to be one of a fragmented world. The student (or teacher) who beholds the world as fragmented sees as relevant only that knowledge which is applicable to the field of specialized interest. He views all else as irrelevant and unnecessary. Therefore, I am proposing that the extent of educational relevance perceived by an individual student is directly proportionate to the dimensions of his world-view. In this light, the ultimate function of a teacher—as distinguished from that of a mere technician—is the progressive enlargement of the student's world of relevancy. This aim, of course, presupposes the progressive enlargement of the teacher's own world.

The curriculum philosophy described above might well call forth the following question: Is not the larger vision actually superfluous in a technological age—that is, shouldn't the dominant educational aim of our industrial society be governed by the efficiency, expediency, and proficiency required by modern technology? To such a question on the critical matter of educating our youth, I would raise another: Should man be taught to be the servant of the technology he has created? Or, put another way, should the economic milieu of the twentieth century prescribe the human horizon?[11]

Around the turn of the century, Edwin Markham gazed upon Millet's painting of "The Brutalized Toiler." Inspired, Markham sat down and composed his world-famous poem, "The Man with the Hoe." This work served to stir up outrage over the inhumanities committed against the physical toilers of Markham's world; yet his inspiration could well symbolize the intellectually brutalized man of the present

[11] Cf. John Kenneth Galbraith, *The New Industrial State*, pp. 398–99; and the general themes developed by Theodore Roszak, *The Making of a Counter Culture*; Lewis Mumford, *The Myth of the Machine: The Pentagon of Power*; and Charles A. Reich, *The Greening of America*.

era. Like Markham, I find myself wondering what revolutionary things might happen if all men were awakened and their potential unleashed. In truth, the supreme challenge to anyone who would be a teacher in this century is nothing short of arousing "the sullen slumber" that characterizes the lives of so many. Again, this labor is one that can be successfully pursued only through the catalytic power of a teacher with vision; anything less will merely perpetuate the apathy and indifference which prevail in so many of our classrooms.

The cries for an educational shake-up are well founded. But simply to tinker with the external structure of our schools will scarcely usher in meaningful change. Such change has to take place in the *internal vision* of each American teacher, for it is here that professional education begins.

Part Two
A Look at Nuts and Bolts

CHAPTER FIVE

FACTS, CONCEPTS, AND GENERALIZATIONS

To extend one's vision to the reaches of philosophy and back to the practical, at-hand matters of classroom teaching and to perceive the intimate connection between the two all in one continuous act of thinking is a heady, mind-expanding experience. I invite the reader to maintain such a perspective as we examine some of the nuts-and-bolts concerns of the professional educator. First, we shall take a look at the pedagogical world of facts, concepts, and generalizations.

"Does anyone in here know what it is to suffer?" Startled, the youthful heads bolted upright with the introductory remarks of the student teacher. Without waiting for a reply, he launched into a dramatic reading of a Civil War battlefield account of terrible human suffering. The initial impact on the class was electric. "He has them!" I thought, as I observed from the back of the class and waited for a lively interchange to develop.

Following the reading, the student teacher plunged into an exposition of facts concerning the comparative life styles of northerners and southerners on the eve of the Civil War. His highly organized lecture was punctuated with chalkboard references. At one point he flashed a map on the wall through an opaque projector so that his students could visualize the regional nature of America in the 1860's. As he presented his data, the student teacher moved up and down the aisles gesturing colorfully with his hands and deliberately changing the inflection of his voice. Overall, his lecture was a dynamic presentation—a notable departure from the more traditional lecture in which a teacher simply stands behind a podium and blandly attempts to convey a body of information to his audience.

The student teacher held to a monologue until the remaining five minutes of the class period. He then queried, "Are there any questions?" There were none and he found himself confronted with an awkward dead spot. Predictably, his students started to engage in all those activities which teen-agers are prone to whenever they find themselves in a boring class situation: they shifted their attention to the clock, banged notebooks shut, started combing their hair, and loudly conversed about matters unrelated to the lesson. When the bell rang, the student teacher dismissed the class with visible relief.

During our follow-up conference, the student teacher expressed great dissatisfaction with himself and also genuine puzzlement about why the class had been so unresponsive. As we talked, it became apparent that his intent had been to involve his students in the lesson through the sheer force and drama of his own personality. By involvement he meant that he wanted his students to think about the facts he had given them, to think about them in a way that would be relevant and meaningful to their own lives.

The student teacher's concerns were understandable since words like "involvement," "relevant," and "meaningful" have come to saturate the vocabulary of professional educators as well as that of American society in general. Moreover, the class had given every indication that they were not involved with his lesson, and that they could not have cared less about the barrage of facts they had been given.

Reliance on the lecture as a primary teaching method embodies definite learning problems. One of the most significant is that people generally hear only 60 to 80 percent of any sustained communication. Consequently, when a teacher rambles on in a classroom, he can safely assume that his students will tune him out a good percentage of the time. The eloquent teacher-speaker of past generations probably had a definite advantage in holding the attention of his audience—that is, in vicariously involving his listeners in whatever he had to say. In the first place, he faced comparatively docile students who were used to being told what to think. In the second place, he had to compete with little intellectual excitement outside the classroom. Thus a teacher who was a fountain of knowledge and a marvelous storyteller stood a good chance of holding his listeners spellbound.

But the advantage enjoyed by good lecturers in the past no longer holds. Today even the most dynamic speaker risks a student reaction which thinks, if not openly says, "We are willing to be taught but not told!"[1]

Provocative questioning is emerging in almost all of man's endeavors. The interaction of people and ideas is creating a situation which rejects the "do-nothings" and demands a vibrant, humanized environment. It's a *now* world with students and teachers alike wanting to be actively involved in making the history of our time.[2]

Furthermore, as painful as the implication may be to a creative, knowledgeable, and polished classroom speaker, today's young people have been reared in front of the television set —a medium through which they have been exposed *ad*

---

[1] "Collision Course in the High Schools," pp. 24–25.

[2] Quoted from a paper written by Karen Fitzpatrick for a graduate course in education, University of Colorado, December, 1969.

nauseam to creative, knowledgeable, and polished speakers.[3] Hence, the teacher who seeks to captivate his students through the vaudeville route and attempts to give them information as a polished performer gives his audience entertainment will find he faces sophisticated "viewers" who are as likely to switch him off in the middle of his classroom performance as readily as they would switch off a television program.

Therefore, the teacher who sees himself as a teller should not be surprised if he does not elicit overt student response. He is, from all outward appearances, projecting a television-like personality—one that may be extremely impressive but nonetheless one that the viewer can relate to only in a one-way passive sense.

In many respects the television set is upstaging the traditional telling role of the classroom teacher. There are even those who argue vehemently that expert televised teaching, backed up with careful staging and exotic props, would be a more effective and less expensive way of conveying information to students than the performance of live teachers. This may be the case, but I believe that *any* medium which simply conveys data in a monologue fashion will be tuned out by today's young people!

There is, in my opinion, a much more fundamental issue surrounding educational "telling," whether the medium is a television set or a flesh-and-blood teacher. That issue is the substantive nature of what is communicated by the teacher in the first place—specifically, how he uses *facts*, *concepts*, and *generalizations*. Since the combination of facts, concepts, and generalizations makes up the "stuff" of the contemporary curriculum (judging from the terminology of the professional

[3] As early as 1955, a leading marketing organization reported that Americans spent more time watching television than they devoted to any other single activity except sleep, and that watching television had become "the most firmly ingrained social habit." Reported by William W. Brickman and Stanley Lehrer, *Automation, Education, and Human Values*, p. 306.

literature, curriculum guides, and methods classes), it seems essential for a teacher to know precisely the meaning of the "stuff" with which he is dealing. As he examines these popular terms, he might well determine that telling and giving are not the only teaching options available to him, and that his major task in reaching an increasingly active generation is not necessarily that of improving his theatrical skills in talking *at* student viewers.

A notable trend in curriculum development is that of encouraging teachers to emphasize concepts and generalizations. This trend undoubtedly has resulted from educational efforts to cope with the geometric increase in knowledge. The intent is not to ignore facts but by concentrating on higher, more abstract levels of knowledge to provide an intellectual framework for better organizing, utilizing, and remembering significant facts. It is as if after centuries of teaching youth in the random manner in which furniture is stored in an attic, educators have discovered that the mental attic has been filled to overflowing with useless bits of junk. Today, in place of junk knowledge, concepts and generalizations are being promoted in order to help conserve thinking space and to give the learner a means of selecting, assessing, and preserving valuable facts amid the dross of experience. In the current curriculum atmosphere of concept development, it is increasingly unfashionable to "just teach facts."[4]

Unfortunately, however, the newly emphasized concepts and generalizations are not at all clear—nor are the facts which they presumably transcend. Yet the lack of clarity has

[4] See, e.g., Marlin L. Tanck, "Teaching Concepts, Generalizations, and Constructs," in *Social Studies Curriculum Development: Prospects and Problems,* ed. Dorothy McClure Fraser, pp. 99–138. See also Colorado Advisory Committee on the Social Studies, *A Guide for Concept Development in the Social Studies,* pp. 1–6; and "Revisions in the Secondary School Curriculum," *University of Colorado Studies Series in Education* No. 3: *Trends in Secondary Education,* pp. 59–96.

not lessened the popularity of this latest curriculum reform. As one critic has suggested, the concept fad is worthy of a parody on a line from the musical *My Fair Lady:* "Educators don't care what they do exactly so long as they pronounce it correctly!"[5]

The above remarks are not intended to poke fun at efforts to move the curricula of our schools away from the conventional practice of filling students with trillions of factual details, a practice which surely is an absurdity in an age of instant-computer recall. Indeed, I champion efforts to encourage teaching and learning at the level of big, general ideas—the only level of thinking, I am convinced, that really makes a whit of a difference in the way human lives are lived. Also, I am most sympathetic to efforts to rise above the alternative posed by our impressive new machinery—that of becoming completely absorbed in the informational phases of education:

. . . we have turned loose our productive genius in the United States to produce a thousand new gadgets which will make it possible to give people more information more rapidly, more effectively, more efficiently than ever before. . . . The genius of computers is that a computer is a marvelous gadget for information storage and retrieval. It is stupid of us to try to make computers out of our students. . . . To try to get them to be people who can store and retrieve information is to attempt to compete with the computers on a ground we will certainly lose. We need to learn to use these events, these gadgets, and to turn our attention to other things. The computer can do a beautiful job of storing information. I suggest that we let them store it and get about the business of doing the things that make us human. It's stupid for us to compete with the computers or to make computers out of students. What we need is to stress the thing that computers can't do—we need to stress our humanism. We need to understand that there is a vast difference between knowing and behaving. Knowing is simply a matter of having some information, but behaving requires the discovery of the meaning of information and is a "people" problem,

[5] Richard Newton, "Concepts, Concepts, Concepts," *Social Education* (January, 1968), p. 41.

and the important aspect of the problem has to do with the discovery of meaning.[6]

It is precisely the need to discover the "meaning of information" in the face of an impossible inundation of facts which is luring many educators toward a focus on concepts and generalizations in the curriculum. But curiously, the search for meaning typically glosses over or completely ignores fundamental philosophic questions about reality and knowledge. Therefore, by the time the idea of emphasizing concepts and generalizations reaches the level of classroom implementation, *what* is to be discovered and the *mechanics* of discovery seldom are questioned in any depth.[7] The frequent result is a promiscuous and utterly meaningless use of concepts and generalizations in the academic setting.

There need not be this curriculum confusion, however, since these two terms do take on important functional meanings *when they are rooted in compatible clusters of basic assumptions about reality and knowledge.* But the crucial point to recognize is that conflicting answers can be provided for each of the seemingly simple questions: What is a fact? What is a concept? What is a generalization? Thus, unless the teacher enjoys flying blind in the classroom or wishes to permit chaos and inconsistency in the development of the "stuff" of his curriculum, he must make conscious personal choices. An examination of the disputed terms within a few philosophic positions will illustrate the *systemic* nature of meaning and some of the choices which are available to the classroom teacher in this matter.

[6] From an address by Arthur W. Combs before the annual conference of the Association for Supervision and Curriculum Development, Dallas, Texas, March, 1967. See also Arthur W. Combs, "Humanizing Education: The Person in the Process," *Humanizing Education: The Person in the Process*, Robert R. Leeper, editor. Washington, D.C.: Association for Supervision and Curriculum Development, 1967, p. 75.

[7] Newton's article, previously cited, is a perceptive analysis of the general curriculum confusion bred by the prevailing superficial treatment of concepts.

LOGICAL POSITIVISM

An educator who espouses the assumptions of a *logical positivist* (or logical empiricist)[8] seeks to *identify the underlying structure in each area of inquiry* according to the best data available to recognized experts at any given time. Here structure refers to a common body of information believed to exist independently of any persons. Positivist structure can be understood in terms of an empirical account of the world—that is, it is physical, biological, and psychological in nature. Held tentatively, the structure nonetheless is regarded as definite information which the learner must acquire in order to be knowledgeable. Phrased in the positivist tradition, concepts provide *the* structure of a subject:

. . . the structure of a discipline is the body of concepts which defines its subject matter and controls research or methods of inquiry into its component parts. The structure of chemistry, for example, consists of the laws and theories of the chemical properties of atoms and molecules.[9]

This notion of concepts was popularized among educators during the 1960's chiefly by Jerome Bruner's *The Process of Education:*

Grasping the structure of a subject is understanding it in a way that permits many other things to be related to it meaningfully. To learn structure, in short, is to learn how things are related.[10]

In other words, a subject is conceived to be a system of "structured" bits of factual data—data which exist *out there.*[11]

---

[8] See, e.g., Herbert Feigl, "Aims of Education for Our Age of Science: Reflections of a Logical Empiricist," in *Modern Philosophies and Education*, ed. Nelson B. Henry, pp. 304–41.

[9] From "Basic Concepts," *Teaching about Communism*, by Richard I. Miller, p. 52. Copyright 1966, McGraw-Hill Book Company. Used with permission of McGraw-Hill Book Company.

[10] Jerome Bruner, *The Process of Education*, Cambridge: Harvard University Press, 1960; paperback Vintage Books, 1960, p. 7.

[11] Cf. comments by Neil Postman and Charles Weingartner, *Teaching as a Subversive Activity*, pp. 77–79.

Rather than clog the learner with the data itself, the teacher puts the student in touch with a set of basic concepts—actually large abstract ideas which are held to be universally applicable. These concepts serve as organizing centers to help the student sort out and classify subsequent factual information. Within this position, the importance of the predetermined underlying structure over factual information itself is sustained. The primacy of structure is illustrated in Richard Miller's recommendation concerning a unit of study on communism: "Historical aspects are important—very important—but they should be used primarily to fill in and bolster basic concepts."[12]

Methodologically, the positivists advocate the "discovery" approach to teaching as a means of having the student learn about a subject in the way authorities perceive the structure of the subject.[13] Discovery, in this sense, implies that a student is taught to see exactly what the experts—via the teacher —want him to see. An excellent example of the nuts-and-bolts implications of this particular approach to concept development is found in Howard Mehlinger's *The Study of Totalitarianism—An Inductive Approach: A Guide for Teachers.* This manual provides the teacher with a complete teaching unit which is

. . . designed to assist students in reaching a sophisticated level of conceptualization. Rather than introducing him to the term [in this unit, the abstract concept "totalitarianism"] and requiring him to define it, the unit sets forth a series of generalizations about totalitarianism so that the student may fashion his own conception of totalitarianism. These generalizations are analogous to building blocks. When the edifice has been constructed, the student should be able to stand back from it and define what he has built; but his definition should have far greater meaning for him than it would have had in the beginning.

[12] Richard I. Miller, "An Approach to Teaching about Communism in Public Secondary Schools," *Phi Delta Kappan* (February, 1962), p. 191.

[13] Cf. Feigl, "Aims of Education," pp. 336–41, and Bruner, *Process of Education*, p. 32.

In addition, each generalization is presented inductively insofar as possible. The teacher is given an activity, a reading, or some visual aid to use in class. Questions are provided which should lead the student to arrive at the generalization on his own. Having "discovered" the generalization for himself, the student is more likely to understand it and to retain it than if he were asked only to memorize what a teacher has told him.[14]

Mehlinger's manual is replete with lesson plans; therefore I have included a sample here. *Lesson Plan A,* which appears on page 101, is a good illustration of positivist assumptions carried out in classroom methodology. The plan is designed on the premise that a concept is "an idea that includes all that is associated with or suggested by a term."[15] In Mehlinger's unit the concept is represented by the abstraction "totalitarianism." An understanding of the following "sub-generalization D" is the obvious objective of the lesson:

Mass manipulation, subordination of the individual and group association, and the use of terror are all means toward an end. In the view of a totalitarian ruler any means can be justified if it moves society closer toward the professed goals.[16]

This sub-generalization is deemed important to know because it is part of nine major generalizations, or "building blocks," which will enable the student to construct a full conception of totalitarianism.

The reader will note three features of *Lesson Plan A:* First, it has been organized to actively involve students in learning through question-asking and discussion; the teacher who utilizes the plan will not conduct a monologue or merely dispense information. Second, the generalization has been established on the basis of expert thinking in *advance* of the lesson. Third, the purpose of the lesson is systematically to *lead* students toward an understanding of the generalization.

---

[14] Howard D. Mehlinger, *The Study of Totalitarianism—An Inductive Approach: A Guide for Teachers* (Washington, D.C.: National Council for the Social Studies, 1965), pp. 6–7.

[15] *Ibid.,* p. 6.

[16] *Ibid.,* p. 86.

LESSON PLAN A[17]

Sub-generalization D [Mass manipulation, subordination of the individual and group association, and the use of terror are all means toward an end. In the view of a totalitarian ruler any means can be justified if it moves society closer toward the professed goals]

Assign *Darkness at Noon* to be read, either in class or at home.

Refer to Stalin's value statement on pages 14–15.

Ask students to define the major Soviet goal in the 1930's.

Discuss consequences arising from the means adopted to achieve this goal.

Students are asked to appraise the justice of the means used to attain rapid industrialization in Russia.

Discuss problem of ends and means in other contexts, encouraging students to suggest goals worthy of any means.

Discuss the threats of totalitarianism within the United States as such threats relate to the dilemma of ends and means.

Lead students to state the generalization.

Estimated time required for this lesson: one day

[17] *Ibid.*, pp. 92–93.

Within the positivist orientation there is sometimes a confusing interchangeability of concepts and generalizations. In Mehlinger's approach, for example, it appears that a mastery of nine major "generalizations" is prerequisite to grasping the "concept" of totalitarianism. Miller, on the other hand, has identified fifteen "basic concepts" which he recommends as a framework for teaching about communism. His designated concepts are very similar in theoretical construct to Mehlinger's generalizations; for example, Miller's seventh concept states, "Communism is a political system that stresses strong and comprehensive control of thought and expression to mold the new Soviet man."[18]

I will leave it to the reader to draw any possible distinctions between concepts and generalizations within the positivist orientation. In my opinion, no real distinction can be made since both concepts and generalizations refer to the *given structure* of an area or discipline. Mehlinger's concept appears to be little more than a symbol which refers to the sum total of his generalizations; consequently, his generalizations provide exactly the same curriculum function as Miller's basic concepts.

In both cases, the underlying assumption is that a *convergence of meanings* is not only possible but highly desirable. The key to the positivist instructional task, therefore, is that of helping the student to discover the given structure for himself. It is this task which unites positivists in their approach to teaching:

Students should be aided and encouraged to *re*discover for themselves some of the simpler and basic facts of modern science; they should be guided toward a fuller understanding of the techniques of observation, measurement, experimentation. . . . Intellectual training that does not fill the mind with relevant subject matter is bound

[18] From "Basic Concepts," *Teaching about Communism*, by Richard I. Miller, p. 9. Copyright 1966, McGraw-Hill Book Company. Used with permission of McGraw-Hill Book Company.

to leave it sterile. "Concepts without content are empty, and those without form are blind."[19]

REALISM

At first glance, it may seem that the educator who is oriented along the lines of *realist* philosophy would be quite comfortable with the teaching approach of a positivist educator. However, in-depth probing reveals some fundamental differences in the meaning the two give to facts, concepts, and generalizations. Like the positivist, the realist holds that facts, concepts, and generalizations exist independently of being known and that the human mind can know what is *out there* as it really is.[20] The realist also shares the positivist's desire to fill the student's mind with important subject matter:

. . . at the beginning they [students] are pure capacities devoid of actual content. The mind of the individual is a blank tablet, as yet uninscribed.[21]

But what needs to be understood is that the realist conceives a view of the world and of man which transcends the positivist's empirical boundaries. Consequently the realist's concepts and generalizations are essentially transempirical in nature. What these terms connote to the realist is best understood in their evolutionary and hierarchical pattern of development: The lowest level of knowledge is the "factual" level. The realist regards facts in the way Aristotle did—as ascertainable

---

[19] Herbert Feigl, "Aims of Education for Our Age of Science: Reflections of a Logical Empiricist," in *Modern Philosophies and Education*, Fifty-fourth Yearbook of the National Society for the Study of Education, ed. Nelson B. Henry (Chicago: The University of Chicago Press, 1955), p. 337.

[20] See, e.g., John Wild, "Education and Human Society: A Realistic View," in *Modern Philosophies and Education*, ed. Nelson B. Henry, pp. 17–56. See also William Oliver Martin, *Realism in Education*, pp. ix, 1–3, 19–57.

[21] Wild, "Education and Human Society," p. 48.

bits of empirical information, or as things "really are" in the world of sensory experience.[22] This meaning of facts is reflected, for example, in W. H. Walsh's description of the qualities of historical fact:

There is an attempt in history, as in perception, to characterize an independent reality . . . we cannot examine the past to see what it was like; but our reconstruction of it is not therefore arbitrary. Historical thinking is controlled by the need to do justice to the evidence, and while that is not fixed in the way some would have us believe, it is nonetheless not made up by the historian. There is something "hard" about it, something which cannot be argued away, but must simply be accepted.[23]

The realist holds that sensory experience has the ability to activate the human mind's inherent capacity to apprehend higher levels of knowledge:

. . . since a human being is *first* of all an animal, however much more he may be potentially, human *experience* is not only prior to the conceptual, but it is much more extensive. The human being has feelings and emotions, likes and dislikes, etc.; he is not merely a "knowing entity" on a conceptual level.

By means of concepts we can grasp and come to know the essential nature of a thing. . . . Unless concepts have some foundation in the nature of things, there could be no conceptual knowledge.[24]

These higher levels of knowledge (or concepts) are grounded in the realist's belief in the existence of a fixed, transempirical, universal pattern of the human good, of the good life—a pattern which abides amid the changing order of empirical reality. When he employs the term "concept," the realist actually is referring to an abstract idea about a *universal form:*

---

[22] It might be helpful for the reader to review the sketch of the classical Aristotelian philosophical tradition in Chapter 3, pp. 52–54.

[23] W. H. Walsh, *Philosophy of History: An Introduction* (New York: Harper & Row, Publishers, 1960), p. 90.

[24] William Oliver Martin, *Realism in Education* (New York: Harper & Row, Publishers, 1969), pp. 164–65.

In classical realism we retain this central principle that the [non-material] forms of things are their most important parts. We hold that the way to know things is by apprehending their forms. But above all, we believe that the forms are *real*, that they are in objects. They are not put there by us, they are not figments of imagination, they are not the products of a culture, they are in things.

What does this view lead to? We take one further step and affirm that human life has a form. It has a law, a natural law. If we could apprehend this natural law, if we could only discern the form of physical nature we would have an insight into the goals and standards appropriate for the good life. That is why the classical realist, when he turns to education, tends to think of it as a means of getting the young, immature person to realize the form inherent in things—to realize his own form and thereby to achieve the good life for himself and mankind.[25]

To a realist, every concept is a notion about the forms—the real, substantial entities of the universe, "existing in themselves and ordered to one another by extramental relations."[26] Based on his belief in potentially common human insight into the way reality "really is"—both its empirical and transempirical dimensions—the realist assumes the possibility of *exact communication* among men and a corresponding *convergence of meaning of universal concepts*. Unless our individual faculties for perceiving reality are distorted for some reason, this process of conceptualizing and communicating about inherent form is regarded as *the way to universal truth*—the means of gaining as complete a perspective of reality as possible.

According to the realist, the highest and most important learning task amounts to synthesizing universal concepts; this synthesizing, and the resulting apprehension of self-evident truths, or generalizations, leads the individual toward an understanding of the pattern of the universe as a whole:

[25] Harry S. Broudy, "A Classical Realist View of Education," in *Philosophies of Education*, ed. Philip H. Phenix (New York: John Wiley & Sons, Inc., 1961), pp. 19–20.

[26] Wild, "Education and Human Society," p. 17. Cf. Martin, *Realism in Education*, pp. 85, 115–16.

The school is . . . the home of those integrative hypotheses and theories where an attempt is made to see things all together as they really are.[27]

The realist educator, therefore, also can call for curriculum reconstruction in which subject matter is selected and developed in terms of large abstractions instead of mere facts. In this case the large abstractions refer to the realist's generalizations: "Some call them 'big ideas,' pervasive ideas like gravitation, or chemical bonds, or the axiomatic basis of mathematics."[28] Because the realist's generalizations are universal, eternal, and immutable in nature, his reconstruction of the curriculum would apply only to the *means* of reaching the highest level of knowledge; the generalizations themselves are not subject to change:

All of this, however different in manner and mode of expression, must be recognized and reflected in the curriculum of any school, at any time, and at any place.[29]

Lesson Plan B, which appears on pages 108–109, represents an effort to convert realist assumptions about reality and knowledge into classroom action. I have constructed the plan from a filmed discussion of a high school physics class.[30] The reader is asked to note three parallels with *Lesson Plan A* insofar as the mechanics of teaching and learning are concerned. Like the first lesson plan, *Lesson Plan B* has been designed to actively involve students through question-asking and discussion. The generalizations surrounding Newton's laws have been established in *advance* of the lesson. And the purpose of this lesson is to *lead* students toward an exact, rigorous understanding of prescribed generalizations. However, in light of the differences in their world and knowledge

[27] Wild, "Education and Human Society," p. 29.

[28] Broudy, "A Classical Realist View," p. 24.

[29] Martin, *Realism in Education*, p. 193. See also Robert Maynard Hutchins, *The Higher Learning in America*, p. 66.

[30] The filmed discussion is reported in "A Classical Realist View of Education," in *Philosophies of Education*, ed. Philip H. Phenix, pp. 22–23.

views, it cannot be assumed that positivist and realist educators will agree on the nature of their generalizations.

Both positivists and realists, it is true, regard existence and reality as identical—that is, both hold that "A is A". Hence efforts to bring about a *convergence of meanings* concerning the "stuff" of learning is an inevitable trademark of the lesson plans of both groups. However, the positivist rejects the notion of a dual reality (an empirical *and* a transempirical world). What is unequivocally *out there* to him is defined by the thinking of experts in various fields, and the experts accumulate the data exclusively through the methods of *empirical science*. The positivist's teaching aim, therefore, is to lead his students toward "stuff" which has been acquired empirically by distinguished researchers.

The realist also relies on empirical data collected by experts —up to a point. Beyond that, in the Aristotelian tradition the realist places a heavy emphasis on the capacity of the *human intellect* (the "mind") to get at what is unequivocally *out there*. Some realists consider *faith* as a still higher means for getting at what is unequivocally *out there*. Consequently, the realist's teaching aim is to lead his students not only to the thinking of experts and the accumulated data of empirical science but to universal truths revealed through the exercise of the student's own intellect (and, for some, also through the development of the student's own supernatural faith).[31] The very content of *Lesson Plan B*, Newtonian physics, reflects the nature of the realist world view: It is a world held together by universal, unchanging natural laws, and one that is perfectly intelligible to the workings of the human intellect.[32]

[31] See discussion of realism in the context of traditional education, Chapter 3, pp. 49–54.

[32] It would be appropriate, at this point, to call the reader's attention to the discussion of quantum mechanics in Chapter 2, pp. 31–34. Werner Heisenberg has argued that *dogmatic realism is the position of classical physics* and as such is incompatible with quantum physics. See Aage Petersen, *Quantum Physics and the Philosophical Tradition*, p. 23. I believe that Heisenberg's analysis is significantly correct in this matter and further suspect that he would apply essentially the same argument to logical positivism.

LESSON PLAN B

Topic: Sir Isaac Newton's three laws of motion

Preparation: Students have been given a reading assignment in their textbook. The lesson discussion for today will be based upon the homework.

Objectives:

1. To understand the nature of the Newtonian laws of motion
2. To apprehend the universality of Newtonian physics

Procedure:

1. Introductory comments by teacher
   a. *Q: Last night when you were reading your assignment on Sir Isaac Newton, how up to date did his ideas seem to you?* (Draw out student reactions.)
   b. Emphasize that Newton lived a long time ago. Suggest that class consider why we bother to study about him today.
   c. Explain that physics lab session will be devoted to a preliminary study of Newton's three laws of motion in an effort to understand how very "modern" his ideas remain.

2. Teacher-led discussion and demonstrations
   a. (Roll ball across lab table.) *Q: From your homework assignment, do you recall which of Newton's laws I am now illustrating?* (Draw out student understanding of law of inertia.)
   b. *Q: Can you explain Newton's second law of motion?* (Draw out student understanding.)

      Q: Can you think of any situations in which this law operates? (E.g., have boys on baseball team explain the fast ball and the slow ball.)
   c. *Q: Can someone explain what Newton's third law really means—i.e., the idea that the action and reaction are equal and opposite?*
      (1) Draw out student understanding.
      (2) Demonstrate with book and lab table: The book as it stands on the table is attracted by the force of gravitation, but the strength of the table resists this force, so the book remains at rest.

3. Brief background lecture by teacher
   a. Recall initial discussion about relevancy of Newton's ideas in the twentieth century.
   b. Point up existence of certain fundamentals and truths in every field of learning: mathematics, science, music, etc.
   c. Point out that Newton discovered the laws which explain why the moon goes around the earth and the planets revolve around the sun.
4. Distribution of *Scientific American* article on rocketry
   a. Have students read article in class.
   b. Follow reading with teacher-led discussion on the application of Newtonian physics to modern rocketry.
5. Have students orally summarize the key Newtonian principles. Explain that class will explore these principles in depth during subsequent meetings.

EXPERIMENTALISM

The curriculum plan of the *experimentalist* (or *pragmatist*) educator also embodies facts, concepts, and generalizations. But in contrast with his positivist and realist colleagues, the experimentalist builds his meanings of these terms upon an intellectual attitude of

. . . relativity, probability, contingency, uncertainty, function, structure as process, multiple causality (or noncausality), non-symmetrical relationships, degrees of difference, and incongruity.[33]

The world, to the experimentalist, is characterized by process and change. Everything that confronts people is in a constant state of movement; however, reality is differentiated in terms of various rates of change. Things which move more slowly, perhaps even giving the appearance of permanence (for example, the Rocky Mountains, the Constitution of the United States, or a nation-state), are regarded as structure. Things which change more rapidly (for example, social norms governing ethical behavior) are regarded as process. However, since everything in existence is viewed as part of the identical on-going, flowing reality, the experimentalist sees no real distinction between structure and process. Although he shares the positivist's rejection of a transempirical order of reality, his world-view is considerably more fluid. He holds that there are *no unchanging substances and no unchanging relations of any kind in the universe*, either in the cosmos as a whole or on the planet earth.

The experimentalist considers man himself to be a fluid creature. Instead of having a fixed, given nature which moves him in certain directions, man is a complex bio-psycho-social organism capable of changing his behavior patterns.

A significant assumption in the experimentalist position is the continuity between the knower and what is known. This

[33] From *Teaching as a Subversive Activity* by Neil Postman and Charles Weingartner, p. 218. Copyright © 1969 by Neil Postman and Charles Weingartner. Used by permission of the publisher, Delacorte Press. See also George R. Geiger, *Philosophy and the Social Order*, pp. 144–52.

involves a rejection of the classic dualism "between an anti-septic and ultimate reality, waiting to be known, and a sentient mind, all ready to infect that reality and distort it into appearance."[34] Instead of beholding a given body of knowledge which exists *out there*, the experimentalist believes that all knowledge is *contextual* in origin. In other words, knowledge emerges as the individual engages in problem-solving, or reflective inquiry.[35]

. . . we have to think—or, at least, are tempted to—when we are confronted with a problem, when some difficulty forces us out of our customary and easier ways of responding. Perplexity, doubt, indecision—these look like the very creators of human thought. Without them, there would be no real occasion to stop daydreaming or to suspect habit and authority; neither would there be any reason to continue thinking when it becomes arduous. Problems not only provide the initial impetus but direct and steady the course of thinking and set up the goal of each process, namely, the solution of the difficulty which stimulated it. Almost any event can act as a motivator of thinking. Whatever sets us to doubting what up to then had been taken for granted is a potential activator. . . .[36]

George Geiger has summarized the key qualities of the experimentalist knowledge-view:

. . . knowledge can be neither discovery nor disclosure of an aloof and already predetermined existence, for the very nature of knowing depends upon a *joint* achievement of organism and environment; so, the knower, as well as the perceived environment, is part of his knowledge; individual differences in knowledge among men can be detected and controlled, eliminated or prized; but the general human element in all knowledge can be neither isolated nor eliminated; scientific knowledge is relative to knowers in specific contexts; thus, what something may be when totally independent

---

[34] George R. Geiger, "An Experimentalist Approach to Education," in *Modern Philosophies and Education*, Fifty-fourth Yearbook of the National Society for the Study of Education, ed. Nelson B. Henry (Chicago: The University of Chicago Press, 1955), p. 138.

[35] See Chapter 3, pp. 47–48, for a detailed description of the reflective method of inquiry.

[36] Geiger, "An Experimentalist Approach," pp. 155–56.

of any observer or frame of reference is a scientifically meaningless question, for knowledge is a *transaction*.[37]

Consequently, when the experimentalist refers to facts, he is referring to *external sensory data as perceived and internalized by the individual learner in the process of responding to a problem*. Since the perception of reality is a highly selective process determined by an individual's background of experience, the experimentalist believes that no two individuals will ever observe the same thing in quite the same way. Therefore, in using "observables" as the basis for testing the truth of factual knowledge, the experimentalist seeks not uniformity but *warranted assertions based on similar findings between people*. In other words, he looks for an approximation of truth, not a convergence of factual interpretations.[38] Because he is very much aware that human bias inevitably enters the perception and interpretation of factual data, he holds all his "truths" conditionally.

Like the positivist and the realist, the experimentalist believes that sensory data activate a higher level of thinking—conceptualization. However, he regards a concept neither as part of an external structure of knowledge nor as a notion about a universal form. To the experimentalist, a concept is *a mental configuration of ideas within the individual* which arises from his examination of facts. Words are merely symbols which arouse mental configurations within the individual. As a person undergoes meaningful experiences, the network of ideas which he associates with certain word symbols expands. Thus the term "concept development" in this philosophic framework denotes *an internal expansion of mental configurations associated with word symbols*:

In their simplest sense, concepts are the ideas to which words refer. . . . For example, the term "culture" has been defined as "the sum of man-made and man-modified artifacts, ideas, and ways of doing things." To a trained anthropologist, this statement of definition is

[37] *Ibid.*, p. 141.
[38] Geiger, *Philosophy and the Social Order*, pp. 167–82.

fairly bursting with meanings. It calls to mind a variety of hunting and fishing weapons used by primitive tribes, courtship and marriage customs, and ideas about religion and morality practiced differently by different peoples. All of these can be tied to the term "culture" because they represent learned behaviors passed on from one generation to the next. The anthropologist can systematize a great deal of what he already knows by formulating short, concise definitions which call to mind a great many facts. He can communicate a great deal to his fellow anthropologists through the use of one word, "culture." However, the intent and meaning of his message would fall on deaf ears if the person for whom it was meant had no experience with a variety of cultures, only an exposure to an academic, verbal definition of word-symbols. The same would be true of other abstractions such as "liberty" and "justice."[39]

Generalizations, to the experimentalist, are the zenith of learning. But unlike the realist, he does not regard these abstractions as self-evident, universal truths. Nor does he regard generalizations in the positivist sense of abstractions about the structure of the physical world which have universal applicability. Consistent with the nature of his facts and concepts, the experimentalist views generalizations as *operational conclusions*—specifically, what the learner *does* with his facts and concepts:

Like concepts, generalizations are short cuts to thinking about the world in which we live. But they are more than that. Generalizations describe relationships. They not only describe data; they give order and meaning to them. . . . Generalizations are synonymous with insight and understanding when they become part of the learner's cognitive structure. This is so when the individual is able to use the new understanding to seek facts or to interpret or assign meaning to new data in his thinking activities. Generalizations are what transfer from intellectual learning activities. Among the most useful generalizations are those which can be stated as "if . . . then" propositions. "If so and so is present, then such and such is likely to happen." Such generalizations help individuals to decide which among the choices open to them they should follow.[40]

[39] Morris R. Lewenstein, *Teaching Social Studies in Junior and Senior High Schools,* © 1963 by Rand McNally & Company, Chicago, p. 84.

[40] *Ibid.*, pp. 85–86.

Stated another way, the experimentalist's generalizations represent the most tenable solution to a problem based on all available evidence. The solution, however, is always tentative; it is never interpreted as a final truth.

What should be apparent at this point is that the experimentalist does not conceive of curriculum "stuff" as givens. Nor does he conceive of his own role as filling the empty minds of students. He hopes, instead, to foster a problematic learning environment—one which breaks in upon the routine experiences of students and prods them to undertake reflective inquiry.[41]

Thinking of generalizing as a highly personal activity can help a teacher guard against forcing students to "learn" generalizations which for them are merely formal verbalisms and call forth no examples or meaning. A generalization developed by others may have no meaning at all for the students who have had no experience with the facts on which it is based. . . . Only through [reflective] thinking will students generalize for themselves. And only if students do generalize for themselves can generalization and understanding come to mean the same thing.[42]

There seems to be divided opinion among experimentalist educators over the precise use of generalizations in the curriculum. Despite the heavy focus on the personal nature of meanings and on the conditionality of all knowledge, Lewenstein, for example, recommends that listings of generalizations "discovered and refined" in the social sciences can serve as "content goals for the social studies curriculum." The following are samples of generalizations which he suggests can be learned from the study of geography:

A commercial economy requires an adequate transportation system. Man's utilization of resources is related to his level of technology.[43]

It appears that Lewenstein's "content goals" for the curriculum would encourage a teaching approach similar to that of

[41] Geiger, "An Experimentalist Approach," p. 156.

[42] Lewenstein, *Teaching Social Studies*, p. 86.

[43] *Ibid.*, p. 85.

the logical positivist, namely, a manipulation of sensory experience in the educational environment with the expectation that the student probably will "discover" the desired generalizations on his own. Such an approach would be consistent with the traditional Deweyite experimentalist view of emphasizing the major *social* aim of education:

. . . the measure of the worth of the administration, curriculum, and methods of instruction of the school is the extent to which they are animated by a social spirit. . . . the school must itself be a community life in all which that implies. Social perceptions and interests can be developed only in a genuinely social medium—one where there is give and take in the building up of a common experience. . . . There is an old saying to the effect that it is not enough for a man to be good; he must be good for something. The something for which a man must be good is capacity to live as a social member so that what he gets from living with others balances with what he contributes.[44]

Lewenstein's approach also is consistent with the experimentalist tradition of giving the weight of authority to the accumulated knowledge of scholars:

The subject matter of education consists primarily of the meanings which supply content to existing social life. *The continuity of social life means that many of these meanings are contributed to present activity by past collective experience.* As social life grows more complex, these factors increase in number and import. There is need of special selection, formulation, and organization in order that they may be adequately transmitted to the new generation. But this very process tends to set up subject matter as something of value just by itself, apart from its function in promoting the realization of the meanings implied in the present experience of the immature. Especially is the educator exposed to the temptation to conceive his task in terms of the pupil's ability to appropriate and reproduce the subject matter in set statements, irrespective of its organization into his activities as *a developing social member*. The positive principle is maintained when the young begin with

[44] John Dewey, *Democracy and Education*, New York: The Macmillan Company, 1916; paperback Free Press, 1966, pp. 358–59. Copyright, The Macmillan Company 1916. Copyright renewed 1944 by John Dewey.

active occupations having a social origin and use, and proceed to a scientific insight in the materials and laws involved, *through assimilating into their more direct experience the ideas and facts communicated by others who have had a larger experience.* [Italics added.][45]

Postman and Weingartner, however, although experimentally oriented, appear to be very critical of the popular modes of experimental inquiry. They suggest that "inquiry" typically amounts to an undesirable seduction of the student:

The inquiry method is very much a product of our electric age. It makes the syllabus obsolete; students generate their own stories by becoming involved in the methods of learning. Where the older school environment has asked, "Who discovered America?" the inquiry method asks, "How do you discover who discovered America?" The older school environments stressed that learning is being told what happened. The inquiry environment stresses that learning is a happening in itself. . . . The goal remains the same: to get into the student's head a series of assertions, definitions, and names as quickly as possible. (This is called "covering content.") The method turns out to be a set of questions posed by the teacher, text, or machine which is intended to lead the student to produce the right answers—answers that the teacher, text, or machine, by gum, knew all the time.[46]

Without negating the teacher's role of *suggesting* things to study, Postman and Weingartner nonetheless insist that an inquiry, regardless of its source, will result in no significant learning unless it is perceived as relevant *by the learner.* They also emphasize that even the most sensitive teacher cannot fully project himself into the perspective of his students,

[45] *Ibid.*, pp. 192–93. The formulation of socially determined generalizations toward which the young are then guided is a procedure that is very much in accord with the traditional experimentalist emphasis on social development. See Appendix A for a further explanation.

[46] From *Teaching as a Subversive Activity* by Neil Postman and Charles Weingartner, pp. 28–29. Copyright © 1969 by Neil Postman and Charles Weingartner. Used by permission of the publisher, Delacorte Press.

and "he dare not assume that his perception of reality is necessarily shared by them."[47] Consequently, Postman and Weingartner focus their attention not on the end product of generalizations but on the intermediate level of concept development. Their goal is to make the student the active producer of his own knowledge. In this task, they propose the elimination of all conventional subject-matter content and advocate the structuring of the entire curriculum around subjective, open-ended questions which will assist the students "to develop and internalize concepts that will help them to survive in the rapidly changing world of the present and the future."[48] The following are samples of the kinds of questions which they deem worthy of answering from the point of view of the students:

What do you worry about most?

What are the causes of your worries?

Can any of your worries be eliminated? How?

Which of them might you deal with first? How do you decide?

Are there other people with the same problems? How do you know? How can you find out?

What, if anything, seems to you to be worth dying for?

How did you come to believe this?

What seems worth living for?

How did you come to believe this?

At the present moment, what would you most like to be—or be able to do? Why? What would you have to know in order to be able to do it? What would you have to do in order to get to know it?

How can you tell "good guys" from "bad guys"?

How can "good" be distinguished from "evil"?

What kind of a person would you most like to be? How might you get to be this kind of person?

[47] *Ibid.*, p. 60.
[48] *Ibid.*, p. 59.

When you hear or read or observe something, how do you know what it means?

Where does meaning "come from"?

What's a "good idea"?

Which of man's ideas would we be better off forgetting? How do you decide?

What is "progress"?

What is "change"?

What kinds of changes are going on right now? Which are important? How are they similar to or different from other changes that have occurred?

What are the relationships between new ideas and change?

Where do *new* ideas come from? How come? So what?

If you wanted to stop one of the changes going on now (pick one), how would you go about it? What consequences would you have to consider?

Of the important changes going on in our society, which should be encouraged and which resisted? Why? How?

What are the dumbest and most dangerous ideas that are "popular" today? Why do you think so? Where did these ideas come from?

What are the conditions necessary for life to survive? Plants? Animals? Humans?

Which of these conditions are necessary for all life?

What are the greatest threats to all forms of life? To plants? To animals? To humans?

How might man's survival activities be different from what they are if he did not have language?

What other "languages" does man have besides those consisting of words?

What would happen, what difference would it make, what would man *not* be able to do if he had no number (mathematical) languages?

What's worth knowing? How do you decide? What are some ways to go about getting to know what's worth knowing?[49]

49 *Ibid.*, pp. 62–65.

Consistent with the experimentalist tradition, Postman and Weingartner's questions are the type that ultimately push a learner toward the level of operational conclusions, or generalizations. Yet such questions place significantly less emphasis (than does the approach of Dewey and Lewenstein) on having students assimilate into their own experience meanings which have been derived by others. Whereas the answering of these and similar questions would require the learner to make rigorous inquiries—frequently into the funded experience of mankind—each question would "allow for alternative answers," "tend to stress the uniqueness of the learner," and would "produce different answers if asked at different stages of the learner's development."[50]

In their provocative book, Postman and Weingartner recommend that the teacher tape a scrap of paper on his bathroom mirror inscribed with the following questions:

What am I going to have my students do today?

What's it good for?

How do I know?[51]

If viewed daily, according to Postman and Weingartner, these three questions will make the teacher much less inclined to follow a prescribed syllabus. They further advise the teacher:

Do not prepare a lesson plan. Instead, confront your students with some sort of problem which might interest them. Then, allow them to work the problem through without your advice or counsel. Your talk should consist of questions directed to particular students, based on remarks made by those students. If a student asks you a question, tell him that you don't know the answer, even if you do. Don't be frightened by the long stretches of silence that might occur. Silence may mean that the students are thinking. Or it may mean that they are growing hostile. The hostility signifies that the students resent the fact that you have shifted the burden of intellectual activity from you to them.[52]

[50] *Ibid.*, p. 66.

[51] *Ibid.*, p. 193.

[52] *Ibid.*, p. 194.

The above advice reflects, probably in a purposely exaggerated fashion, Postman and Weingarter's extreme opposition to curriculum givens of any variety. However, I would point out that the experimentalist philosophy of education— even the questions curriculum advocated by Postman and Weingartner—does not imply an automatic rejection of advance lesson planning.[53] What does appear to be rejected is the more traditional lesson plan format in which students are *led* to predetermined meanings of facts, concepts, and generalizations:

The only kind of lesson plan, or syllabus, that makes sense . . . is one that tries to predict, account for and deal with the authentic responses of learners to a particular problem: the kinds of questions they will ask, the obstacles they will face, their attitudes, the possible solutions they will offer, etc. Thus, he is rarely frustrated by "wrong answers," false starts, irrelevant directions. These are the stuff of which his best lessons and opportunities are made.[54]

Although differences in degree seem to exist among experimentalist educators, the hallmark of this philosophy is that it encourages students to become personally responsible for securing their own answers; "it is not a question of accepting or not accepting what somebody else believes."[55]

In *Lesson Plan C*, which appears on pages 122–124, I have sought to construct a lesson which embodies experimentalist assumptions. The reader will note some distinguishing characteristics: First, the lesson is designed to confront the student with a disturbing problem, one which is likely to jar him into personal involvement. Second, the student is asked to work through his own thinking about the problem but is advised that his conclusions will necessarily be incomplete and tem-

[53] I invite the reader to study my own argument for advance planning— whatever one's educational philosophy—in Appendix B.

[54] Postman and Weingartner, *Teaching as a Subversive Activity*, pp. 35–36.

[55] H. Gordon Hullfish, "An Experimentalist View of Education," in *Philosophies of Education*, ed. Philip H. Phenix (New York: John Wiley & Sons, Inc., 1961), p. 14.

porary. Third, the obvious aim of the lesson is to prod the student toward operational conclusions (generalizations) of his own, but only after he has made a careful examination of available factual data. Fourth, the lesson has a built-in means for giving the teacher at least a feel for concept development: He can compare the breadth and depth of student understanding expressed in the introductory discussion of the *Code of Conduct* with a possible expansion of student ideas following the *Life* reading, and ultimately with the ideas reflected in the students' oral and written reports. Fifth, the pivotal questions employed in the lesson and in the follow-up assignment are open-ended and divergent; they will tend to generate additional questions and problems, and they will lend themselves to a plurality of meanings.

Some experimentalists might find *Lesson Plan C* too teacher-directed, and would prefer to organize learning activities more in response to student-created problems. This is likely to be the posture of Neil Postman and Charles Weingartner. However, many experimentalist teachers regard their professional responsibility as one of organizing, selecting, and directing learning activities in order that student participation—whether on a group or individual basis—will be fostered with a maximum of individual understanding and growth.[56] Such a view of the teaching role reflects John Dewey's idea that the business of education is to replace chance activities with activities selected to guide learning.[57] Dewey's belief that the teacher has an obligation to stimulate and direct interest has been incorporated in *Lesson Plan C*.

[56] See, e.g., the role of the experimentalist teacher as described by Hullfish, *ibid.*, p. 12.

[57] Dewey, *Democracy and Education*, p. 274.

LESSON PLAN C

Date: January 6, 1970

Topic: The Mylai incident in Vietnam

Objectives:

1. To develop skill in drawing conclusions from a collection of information and opinions

2. To develop an understanding of the kinds of value judgments involved in formulating American foreign policy

3. To develop an understanding of the moral problems confronting America in connection with the conduct of the Vietnam conflict

4. To develop a sense of personal responsibility in giving meaning to abstract principles

Procedure:

1. Introduce lesson by displaying United States Army poster (No. DOD P-9 VI; DA Poster 21–100–6) illustrating point VI of the military Code of Conduct:

   "I will never forget that I am an American fighting man, responsible for my actions, and dedicated to the principles which made my country free. I will trust in my God and in the United States of America."

2. Ask students to interpret what the Code of Conduct means to them:

   Q: What, to you, are the "principles" which made this country free?

   Q: If you were in uniform today, what specific actions would you feel personally responsible for?

   Q: How would you go about deciding whether your behavior was "right" or "wrong"?

3. Distribute reprints of the controversial *Life* magazine article of December 5, 1969, "The Massacre at Mylai."

   a. Have students read article in class.

   b. Ask students to reconsider above questions against the *Life* presentation of the Mylai incident.

Q: How accurate is the Life *account of this incident? How will you decide the validity of its charges against the American soldiers?*

Q: What relationship is there between the Mylai incident and the case of Adolph Eichmann?

Q: What is your opinion about the responsibility of these soldiers for their purported actions?

4. Present brief background lecture.

   a. Point out that in an age of rapid communications, citizens of a democracy are swamped with information from many sources—TV, radio, newspapers, magazines, books—about each crisis or conflict or event which occurs in an ever-shrinking world.

   b. Explain that sifting through this mass of information in order to understand it is the necessary though difficult task of each one of us.

   c. Point out that the *Life* article does not represent a complete set of data about this incident. Therefore our conclusions will necessarily be incomplete and temporary—open to the examination of additional data.

   d. Emphasize the desirability of developing the habit of looking into many sources of information in order to equip ourselves to reach intelligent decisions and conclusions about events in this rapid-moving, sometimes confusing world.

   e. Point out that whereas we will probably never know exactly what happened at Mylai, many sources of information can give us a larger picture of the event than reliance on a single point of view.

5. Make assignment.

   a. Explain to class that each student will have one week in which to prepare a full report on the Mylai incident. The report is to be written in the form of a "briefing" to a "superior officer" who is largely ignorant of what transpired at Mylai. He will have to make decisions on the basis of what each student advises him, so the report should explore the background as well as the present developments concerning the incident.

b. Distribute to each student a packet of twenty mimeographed articles on the Mylai incident from a wide range of periodicals. Suggest that the students use the various articles to help sift out facts and opinions as they write the report. Advise students that they are free to use *any* additional materials—at school or at home—to complete their reports.

c. Distribute and review with class a mimeographed sheet listing the following guideline questions for their use in examining the issue and in preparing their reports:

(1) Why are American military forces fighting in Vietnam?

(2) What seem to be the basic issues of the Vietnam conflict?

(3) What influence might public opinion have on the conduct of the war?

(4) What seem to be the facts of the Mylai incident?

(5) What is your evaluation of *Life* magazine's charge of "the deliberate slaughter of old men, women, children, and babies"?

(6) What is your evaluation of your other sources of information? What is the basis for your evaluation?

(7) To what extent do you believe the American soldiers were responsible for the events at Mylai?

(8) Based on your interpretation of data examined up to this time, what should be America's official policy regarding the Mylai incident?

6. Advise students to bring their written reports to class one week from today. Also, advise them to be prepared at that time to share their thinking on this issue in an informal class discussion.

EXISTENTIALISM

As the reader probably has surmised, my own view of facts, concepts, and generalizations—and my resulting approach to lesson planning—are sympathetic to the experimentalist position. But the particular interpretation I bring to the "stuff" of curriculum needs to be qualified within my theistic orientation to *existentialism*.

I share with the experimentalist the belief that the meanings of facts, concepts, and generalizations cannot be separated from the perceptual framework of the individual human being. I also share the experimentalist's insistence that students must be encouraged to become personally responsible for securing their own answers. I agree with Postman and Weingartner that shifting the burden of thought to students can be a painful—even unbearable—experience for them.[58] This kind of apprehension, I am convinced, with no guarantees of personal success and fraught with the insecurities of not knowing the results of all our strivings, is a prerequisite to learning —for me, for my students, for anyone. But despite these general areas of agreement, I do stand apart from the experimentalist in several important respects:

First, as I have stated elsewhere,[59] I place a much greater emphasis on the subjective learner than does the experimentalist. This subjectivity would color, for example, the attitude behind my own use of *Lesson Plan C*. Whereas I would be quite comfortable in organizing, selecting, and directing learning activities and in stimulating interest, the purpose of such instructional leadership would not be to guide students in the experimentalist sense. It is important to keep in mind a differentiation between the experimentalist and existentialist world-views in this matter of guiding students. The former view is built on the assumption of *social evolution*—a natural and progressive adaptation by individuals to the common

[58] See Postman and Weingartner, *Teaching as a Subversive Activity*, p. 194.

[59] See Chapter 3, pp. 54–55, and Appendix A.

aims, beliefs, and aspirations of the total society.[60] The experimentalist teacher, therefore, is likely to be interested in guiding his students so that they will "see" what he regards as natural for them to see: the progressive development of normative social behavior based on mutual understanding and an identity of interests with other members of society. Thus, a plurality of student meanings within the experimentalist position needs to be understood as having *socially determined parameters;* and however broadly these might be conceived, parameters define human limits.

By way of contrast, the existentialist world-view is not tied to an assumption of social evolution. Progress, or lack thereof, is interpreted by the existentialist in terms of what each individual chooses to make of his own life. Thus my guidance functions are perceived in the sense of planning learning activities that will encourage the individual student to "see" himself. Because of my commitment to the uniqueness of each human being, I regard the plurality of student meanings which might be evoked in the course of learning activities as having *no definable parameters.*

Second, I refuse to be bound to an empirical delimitation of reality; consequently, my concepts and generalizations are not necessarily restricted to naturalistic meanings nor to tests of validity which rely on sensory evidence.

Third, although I have a healthy respect for the influence of environmental factors on human lives, I do not believe that the physical environment is all-determining in the way an individual perceives his world and internalizes meaning thereof. In the existentialist spirit, I hold that a human being has the capacity intellectually and emotionally to *transcend* his particular physical environment. This is not to ignore man as a bio-psycho-social organism; it is to suggest that he is potentially *more* than a complex physical entity. It is precisely the struggle which exists between the shaping influence of a given environment and the individual's efforts to break away from that influence which produces the tension

[60] See Appendix A.

that is *necessary* to help him become a free and fully functioning person. Only as an individual transcends his environment does he become *self-determining and ultimately unpredictable.*[61]

Fourth, I shun the experimentalist (at least the Deweyite) focus on the individual as a member of a larger unit, "society," and the resulting concern for improving society by improving social institutions. Instead, I see society as a collection of individuals, each of whom is unique and irreplaceable. I hold that in order to fulfill himself as a unique being, each person must be conscious of himself as a responsible agent—not as an instance of a universal or generalized group called "society as a whole." Translated to the educational setting, this implies the fundamental belief that no individual can learn if he is regarded simply as part of a group, as a unit in society. He must be regarded as a special self. Therefore, if society is to be improved through education, the improvement must necessarily begin with individual selves, not with groups or "institutions" at large.

Fifth, I am more wary than the experimentalist of the authority frequently posed by "others who have had larger experience." This is not to say that I choose to ignore the accumulated knowledge of scholars, but I am convinced that experiential evidence is not the *summum bonum* of truth. Thus I refuse to reduce all of human existence to this external and observable criterion of validity.

Sixth, I would place even greater emphasis than the experimentalist upon the technique of confronting students with disturbing problems in the learning situation. This is consistent with the existentialist emphasis on *disquietude* and *crisis* as the origin of personal awareness. Methodologically, I find an open-ended, reflective method of inquiry very useful in creating a sense of crisis. However, unlike the experimentalist, I would not insist that the student's end result (his generalization) be public, verifiable, and sharable. This pos-

[61] Cf. Sidney M. Jourard, "A Psychology of Transcendent-Behavior," *Disclosing Man to Himself*, pp. 204–210.

ture of mine is not an arbitrary one; I simply choose to think that there are realms of knowledge and avenues of thought that lend themselves to transempirical forms of reasoning and to intuitive processes.[62]

Seventh, I do not regard all reality as a fluid process; instead, I choose to believe in a realm of permanence. By the same token, I do not believe that all values regarding the good, the true, and the beautiful simply "emerge" in a context relative to space and time. But I do consider that *all meanings*—whether of things and events perceived from the concrete world of physical reality, or whether of universal ideas apprehended from a transempirical order of reality—are inextricably bound up with the existence of individual selves. Since no two selves are identical (physically, emotionally, mentally, or spiritually), I believe that educational quests for identical meanings of facts, concepts, and generalizations are grossly misplaced efforts. I hold, instead, that the discovery of meaning must be an internal process, not one to be hammered out in curriculum committees nor even among the most sophisticated scholars.

At the same time, I hold that the lack of identical meanings on the "stuff" of learning need not prevent us from trying to find and share *degrees* of similarity in our personal meanings. After all, the degrees of similarity in meaning which we bring to the word symbols describing our various interpretations of reality enable us to communicate with each other in the first place. I am merely suggesting that we would vastly improve our mutual understandings if—in our educational efforts as well as in our other human endeavors—we would be satisfied to look only for areas of possible overlapping in our respective meanings and resign ourselves to very real differences in viewpoints wherever no overlapping occurs. This view calls for a cessation of searches for a universal "fit" for any and all ideas. In this recommendation, I am fully in accord with Postman and Weingartner:

[62] Cf. the speculative-intuitive approaches to knowledge discussed in Chapter 3, pp. 58–63.

. . . since our perceptions come from us and our past experience, it is obvious that each individual will perceive what is "out there" in a unique way. We have no common world, and communication is possible only to the extent that two perceivers have similar purposes, assumptions, and experience. The process of becoming an effective social being is contingent upon seeing the other's point of view.[63]

Invariably, group efforts to discover uniform and universally applicable meanings (however fixed or tentative these may be) fall into the old formula: If you do not agree that what we say is correct, you are wrong! When one human being relates to another with the superior-inferior attitude of "You are wrong," he thereby snuffs out part of the other's right to existence. He also manifests sublime ignorance of the probable richness and vitality of the other's perception of reality and knowledge. The better way to educate, I prefer to think, is to provide the opportunities, stimulation, and encouragement to help a student expand his vision in his own way.

On the following pages, I have provided a sample outline for a teaching unit. This topical outline—actually no more than a content listing—is the preliminary stage of a full teaching unit (which would also consider specific methodology). I have developed this unit outline around the concept of equality. It is intended to illustrate a teaching approach consistent with my own existentialist orientation. I have used a unit format (instead of a daily lesson plan) in order to demonstrate concept development over a period of time. Lesson plans, of course, would be derived from the unit outline.

As the reader will observe, no attempt has been made in the sample unit to "cover information." Content has been selected and organized in terms of its relevancy to the focal point of the unit, namely the expansion of the student's concept of equality. Whatever other content on the Greeks, the Romans, etc., might conceivably be studied has been reserved

[63] From *Teaching as a Subversive Activity* by Neil Postman and Charles Weingartner, p. 90. Copyright © 1969 by Neil Postman and Charles Weingartner. Used by permission of the publisher, Delacorte Press.

for *other* units—if, indeed, such information is deemed significant in the development of other concepts.

As the reader also will note, the unit has been designed deliberately to expose the student to conflicting, disturbing ideas through extensive use of original source material. The assumption is that a student is not likely to examine, for example, the views on equality espoused by the Black Panthers, George Wallace, Martin Luther King, Cesar Chavez, and Lester Maddox, among others, and still feel placid about the matter.

Items 12 (j), (k), and (l) listed in the sample unit have been selected for their direct relevancy to students living in the metropolitan area of Denver, Colorado, at the time of this writing.

Instead of structuring this social studies unit around the conventional, chronological, building-block formula, I have organized it to initially involve the student from his own point in time—*the present*. The purpose of the subsequent examination of selected historical data is to develop the student's awareness of the many highly complicated meanings of human equality today.

The source material for the unit—although ostensibly a history lesson—is interdisciplinary. Under the assumption that life itself is a whole piece of cloth, the sacred lines of academic disciplines have been crossed freely.

Finally, the unit is intended to culminate with activities that encourage the student to make his own generalizations on the basis of his expanded, internalized network of ideas (or concept) of equality. It is anticipated that what equality "means" and what it "ought to mean" will evoke from a group of students many different conclusions.

SAMPLE UNIT OUTLINE: THE STRUGGLE FOR EQUALITY

Objectives:

1. Understanding of the consequences of ideas and events on human lives
2. Understanding of the diverse, conflicting meanings of human equality
3. Understanding of the impact of past ideas and events regarding human relationships on the present social order
4. Understanding of the relationships between ideas on human nature and the ordering of human society
5. Understanding of the effect of racial and economic ideas on the ordering of human society
6. Understanding of the influence of the multidimensioned American ideological heritage on the present social revolution

Content outline:

1. What do we mean by equality? Its role in our lives today?
2. What do we mean by the American cultural heritage?
3. Analysis of the Greek social thought
   a. Case study of Plato's *The Republic* (theory of metals)
   b. Case study of Aristotle's theory of the ideal social order
4. Analysis of the Roman social order
   a. Era of the Roman republic (patricians, plebeians, slaves)
   b. Era of the Roman empire (emperor, citizens, slaves)
5. Analysis of the social thought of medieval Europe—doctrine of Corpus Christianum
   a. Case study of St. Augustine's *The City of God*
   b. Analysis of feudalism as a social system (clergy, lords, serfs)
6. Renaissance nation-building in Western Europe (theories of the divine right of monarchy)
   a. Case study of Machiavelli's *The Prince*
   b. Case study of Louis XIV and the French Bourbon regime (absolute monarchy and subjects)

7. The Enlightenment era

   a. Comparison of the social thought of John Locke and Jean Jacques Rousseau (natural aristocracy versus the noble savage)

   b. Case studies of the social thought of early Americans

      (1) Alexander Hamilton (aristocracy of wealth)
      (2) Thomas Jefferson (aristocracy of talent)
      (3) Andrew Jackson (egalitarian spirit)

8. Impact of the Industrial Revolution on the social order

   a. Analysis of the European Revolutions of 1848

      (1) "Bourgeoisie" and "proletariat"
      (2) J. Hampden Jackson's *Marx, Proudhon, and European Socialism*

   b. Case studies of the American Labor movement

      (1) The Homestead and Pullman strikes
      (2) Upton Sinclair's *The Jungle*
      (3) Marcia Davenport's *The Valley of Decision*
      (4) Eugene Debs and American socialism
      (5) Samuel Gompers and the American Federation of Labor

9. Impact of Charles Darwin on nineteenth-century sociological thought

   a. Analysis of *The Origin of the Species*
   b. Herbert Spencer and "survival of the fittest"
   c. William Graham Sumner, *The Absurd Effort to Make the World Over*
   d. Stewart H. Holbrook, *The Age of the Moguls*
   e. Frederick Lewis Allen, *The Lords of Creation*

10. Impact of nineteenth- and twentieth-century doctrines of racism on the social order and concept of equality

    a. Analysis of global patterns of nineteenth-century Western imperialism

    b. Rudyard Kipling and "the white man's burden"

    c. Case studies of European and American racists:

       (1) George Fitzhugh, *Sociology for the South or the Failure of Free Society* (American Civil War era)
       (2) Count Arthur de Gobineau, *Essay on the Inequality of the Human Races* (France)

(3) Houston Stewart Chamberlain, *Foundations of the Nineteenth Century* (England, Germany)

(4) Madison Grant, *The Passing of the Great Race* (America)

(5) Lothrop Stoddard, *The Rising Tide of Color* (America)

(6) Adolph Hitler, *Mein Kampf* (Germany)

d. Analysis of American immigration laws from 1882 to date

11. Consequences of post–World War II revolution of rising expectations

a. Analysis of the Four Freedoms

b. Analysis of the Preamble of the United Nations Charter

c. Analysis of the thinking of mid-twentieth-century social scientists on the human social order

(1) UNESCO pamphlet series, "The Race Question in Modern Science"

(a) Juan Comas, *Racial Myths*

(b) L. C. Dunn, *Race and Biology*

(c) Michel Leiris, *Race and Culture*

(d) Claude Levi-Strauss, *Race and History*

(e) Arnold Rose, *The Roots of Prejudice*

(2) Ashley Montagu, *Man's Most Dangerous Myth: The Fallacy of Race*

(3) Clyde Kluckhohn, *Mirror for Man*

(4) L. C. Dunn and T. Dobzhansky, *Heredity, Race, and Society*

(5) Benjamin Quarles, *The Negro in the Making of Modern America*

(6) Leonard Irvin, *Minorities in the United States*

(7) Charles Silberman, *Crisis in Black and White*

(8) Michael Harrington, *The Other America*

(9) Ben H. Bagdikian, *A New Report on the Poor in America*

d. *Life* magazine (March 8, 1968), "The Negro and the Cities —The Cry that Will Be Heard."

e. U.S. Riot Commission Report, *Report of the National Advisory Commission on Civil Disorders* (Kerner Report)

12. Analysis of contemporary viewpoints on human equality

a. Case study of War on Poverty programs

b. Case study of George Wallace

   c. Case study of Louise Day Hicks

   d. Case study of Stokely Carmichael

   e. Case study of Martin Luther King

   f. Case study of James Groppi

   g. Case study of Black Panthers

   h. Case study of Cesar Chavez

   i. Case study of Lester Maddox

   j. Case study of Crusade for Justice

   k. Case study of the 1967 Denver School Bond issue

      (1) Stephen Knight
      (2) A. Edgar Benton

   l. Case study of the 1968–1970 Denver Public Schools integration (mandatory versus voluntary busing)

      (1) Rachel Noel
      (2) Robert Gilbert
      (3) James Perrill

13. Equality in America—what it means; what it ought to mean. Summary and conclusions.

CHAPTER SIX

OBJECTIVES AND OBJECTIVES

During the past several years the world of education has been engulfed by a new tidal wave of change—the mandatory writing of "behavioral objectives" by teachers and the planning of learning activities and evaluation procedures in the light of those objectives. Classroom teachers are being advised by powerful educational voices to include only those learnings which in some way can be *measured.*

If my own graduate students from districts throughout the sprawling Denver metropolitan area are accurate weather vanes of public school teachers across this country, then increasing numbers of teachers are being confronted with serious personal dilemmas. Some teachers, neither articulate enough to protest nor secure enough to follow the dictates of their own convictions, simply allow themselves to be swept along by the external directives on how and what to teach. Some, whose feeble cries about "ignoring other kinds of learning" are met with scorn, incredulity, and/or insistence that the problem of getting at presently "unmeasurable learn-ings" *ultimately will be resolved by experts,* rationalize their helplessness and question no further. The few who refuse to passively succumb to administrative fiat or who resign in frustration are learning to play a new game of professional survival. "I refuse to sell my soul over this behavioral ob-jective ruling," one troubled educator told me recently, "so I write two sets of lesson plans: One set satisfies the front office, and one set enables me to live with myself in the class-room." A regrettable waste of a teacher's valuable time, but the practice is understandable when a monistic orientation is imposed upon a pluralistic staff.

As in the case of virtually all other educational matters, the justification for using behavioral objectives as a design for learning[1] is *philosophically systemic in nature.* Consequently, unless a teacher espouses the basic assumptions compatible with behavioral objectives, he is likely to find himself wearing a curriculum hair shirt! This fact tends to be overlooked in the vast bulk of contemporary curriculum deliberations. And the oversight is not restricted to the public schools. Failure to relate learning objectives to philosophic assumptions can be found in pronouncements and directives coming from high and influential places: the United States Office of Education,[2] state departments of education, universities that prepare school social workers,[3] and federal and state funding agen-

---

[1] The focus on objectives throughout this chapter is in relationship to their functional use in structuring unit and lesson plans. The reader will note that statements of purpose, or objectives, precede a descrip-tion of the introductory, developmental, and culminating activities in the sample unit and lesson plans which appear in Chapter 5. (It also should be noted that none of the objectives written as part of those sample plans is behavioral in formulation.)

[2] E.g., see Sue M. Brett, "The Federal View of Behavioral Objectives," in *On Writing Behavioral Objectives for English,* ed. John Maxwell and Anthony Tovatt, pp. 43–47.

[3] E.g., see Frank Maple, "Treatment by Objectives: Preliminary Draft of a Program to Train Workers to Write and Adapt Treatment Ob-jectives."

cies.[4] It is apparent that even many teacher education institutions send their graduates out into the field without having exposed them to the barest notion of the relationship between learning objectives and fundamental questions on the basic nature of man and knowledge itself.

It is not my intention here to wage a war against behavioral objectives per se. For years, it is true, teachers of integrity have employed behavioral-type objectives in their classroom situations. I insist upon sustaining such individual integrity, and if these teachers can obtain the help of experts in tightening up the writing of their objectives, so much the better for them. However, I *am* throwing down the gauntlet before anyone who ignores professional *choice* in this matter. And I *am* charging serious irresponsibility among many educational leaders for their blindness to the existence of the nonbehavioristic outlook described, for example, by Theodore Roszak:

. . . the primary purpose of human existence is not to devise ways of piling up ever greater heaps of knowledge, but to discover ways to live from day to day that integrate the whole of our nature by way of yielding nobility of conduct, honest fellowship, and joy. And to achieve those ends, a man need perhaps "know" very little in the conventional, intellectual sense of the word. But what he does know and may only be able to express by eloquent silence, by the grace of his most commonplace daily gestures, will approach more closely to whatever reality is than the most dogged and disciplined intellectual endeavor. For if that elusive concept "reality" has any meaning, it must be that toward which the entire human being reaches out for satisfaction, and not simply some fact-and-theory-mongering fraction of the personality. What is important, therefore, is that our lives be as *big* as possible, capable

[4] E.g., see *Teacher Corps Policy and Related Instructions for Proposal Development*, p. 19: "All new programs are requested to develop a flexible, preservice training program around specified performance competencies which will be expected of interns before they enter the inservice phase of the program. . . . Such a program design includes: That specific objectives be defined for interns, team leaders, and staff; *that these objectives be defined in performance or behavioral terms* by the university and school districts together; that alternative means of reaching these objectives be provided."

of embracing the vastness of those experiences which, though yielding no articulate, demonstrable propositions, nevertheless awake in us a sense of the world's majesty.

The existence of such experiences can hardly be denied without casting out of our lives the witness of those who have been in touch with such things as only music, drama, dance, the plastic arts, and rhapsodic utterance can express. How dare we set aside as a "nothing but," or a "merely," or a "just" the work of one artist, one poet, one visionary seer, without diminishing our nature? For these, as much as any scientist or technician, are our fellow human beings. And they cry out to us in song and story, in the demanding beauty of line, color, shape, and movement. We have their lives before us as testimony that men and women have lived—and lived magnificently—in communion with such things as the intellective consciousness can do no justice to. If their work could, after some fashion, be explained, or explained away, if it could be computerized—and there are those who see this as a sensible project—it would overlook the elemental fact that in the making of these glorious things, these images, these utterances, these gestures, there was a supreme joy, and that the achievement of that joy was the purpose of their work. In the making, the makers breathed an ecstatic air. The technical mind that by-passes the making in favor of the made has already missed the entire meaning of this thing we call "creativity" . . . . What *is* of supreme importance is that each of us should become a person, a whole and integrated person in whom there is manifested a sense of having come to terms with a reality that is awesomely vast.[5]

Lest the reader consider historian Roszak's subjectivity a sharp departure from "modern scientific thought" (essentially his refutation of the objectivity, causality, and determinism which color behavioristic analyses of human life and human learning), I refer him to mathematician Banesh Hoffmann's fascinating discussion of the scientific and philosophic implications of quantum mechanics:

. . . the universe is more than a collection of objective experi-

[5] From *The Making of a Counter Culture* by Theodore Roszak, copyright © 1968, 1969 by Theodore Roszak. Anchor Books edition, pp. 233–35. Reprinted by permission of Doubleday & Company, Inc. and Faber and Faber Ltd.

mental data; more than the complexus of theories, abstractions, and special assumptions devised to hold the data together; more, indeed, than any construct modeled on this cold objectivity. For there is a deeper, more subjective world, a world of sensation and emotion, of aesthetic, moral, and religious values as yet beyond the grasp of objective science. And towering majestically over all, inscrutable and inescapable, is the awful mystery of Existence itself, to confound the mind with an eternal enigma.[6]

Although Roszak did not single out teachers nor the trend toward behavioral objectives in his work, he nonetheless hit the fundamental problem squarely:

In the technocracy everything aspires to become purely technical, the subject of professional attention. The technocracy is therefore the regime of experts—or of those who can employ the experts. . . . it is characteristic of the technology to render itself ideologically invisible. Its assumptions about reality and its values become as unobtrusively pervasive as the air we breathe. While daily political argument continues within and between the capitalist and collectivist societies of the world, the technocracy increases and consolidates its power in both as a trans-political phenomenon following the dictates of industrial efficiency, rationality, and necessity. In all these arguments, the technocracy assumes a position similar to that of the purely neutral umpire in an athletic contest. The umpire is normally the least obtrusive person on the scene. Why? Because we give our attention and passionate allegiance to the teams, who compete within the rules; we tend to ignore the man who stands above the contest and who simply interprets and enforces the rules. Yet, in a sense, the umpire is the most significant figure in the game, since he alone sets the limits and goals of the competition and judges the contenders. . . . To a mournfully great extent, the progress of expertise, especially as it seeks to mechanize culture, is a waging of open warfare upon joy. It is a bewilderingly perverse effort to demonstrate that nothing, *absolutely nothing* is particularly special, unique, or marvelous, but can be lowered to the status of mechanized routine. More and more the spirit of

[6] From *The Strange Story of the Quantum* by Banesh Hoffmann, Dover Publications, Inc., New York, 1959, pp. 189–90. Reprinted through permission of the publisher. (Also see earlier discussion of the quantum theory in Chapter 2, pp. 31–34.)

"nothing but" hovers over advanced scientific research: the effort to degrade, disenchant, level down.[7]

It is the current national preoccupation with the systems approach to education (actually an extension of the above-described technocratic mentality) which has accorded behavioral objectives a feverish priority and an exclusive status.[8] The educational technocrats view objectives couched in "glittering generalities" as root causes of sloppy teaching and inefficient learning, and hold that such curriculum guidelines are no guidelines at all. To remedy this situation, they look to industrial procedures for processing raw materials with a minimum of waste and with built-in quality controls. Reflecting the "nothing but" regard for knowledge and knowing, behavioral objectives presumably afford the entire education industry with precise means for determining its productivity.

At a time when American taxpayers are demanding a clear assessment of mounting educational costs, behavioral objectives have an understandable appeal. They facilitate the compiling of what amounts to a profit-and-loss statement on the performance of students over specific periods of time and at established grade levels. In a word, they harmonize beautifully with growing calls for financial accountability—an accountability which itself is deeply colored by the prevailing mechanistic-materialist culture. And this culture, it must be re-emphasized, still is steeped in the mode of thought characteristic of classical Newtonian science: it assumes that man has the capacity to understand, predict, and ultimately control all the phenomena of nature, including human life itself. Stated simply, *the mechanistic-materialist culture tolerates no random element of behavior in individual human lives.*[9] What has

[7] From *The Making of a Counter Culture* by Theodore Roszak, copyright © 1968, 1969 by Theodore Roszak. Anchor Books edition, pp. 7, 8, 229. Reprinted by permission of Doubleday & Company, Inc.

[8] The reader may wish to refer to earlier discussion of the systems approach in Chapter 1, pp. 16–17.

[9] Again, see earlier discussion of the random element of behavior in relationship to quantum mechanics in Chapter 2, pp. 31–34.

yet to be seriously challenged in contemporary America (except for a few scholars like Roszak and the disenchanted youth of the nontechnocratic counter culture) is the *thesis that human accountability in terms of measurable results and a publicly verifiable profit-and-loss statement is necessary,* and even that such human accountability is *possible!*

I submit that the behavioral objective crusade has seduced many an educator into a particular philosophic orientation, negating the legitimacy of metaphysical, epistemological, and axiological views which do not fit the prescribed teaching formula. We can appreciate the seriousness of the problem by examining behavioral objectives at their foundational level and by contrasting these objectives with nonbehavioristic modes of thought. As we explore this issue further, I invite my reader to recall the relationship drawn in Chapter 4 between basic philosophic assumptions and learning theories.[10] This wholistic relationship is necessary to keep in mind since curriculum disputes regarding learning objectives seldom go beyond a psychological level of consideration—if, indeed, they go even that far. I also invite him to keep in mind the differing connotations of facts, concepts, and generalizations explored in Chapter 5. The formulation of learning objectives is not an isolated curriculum problem. It is, instead, a definite outgrowth of how one sees the "stuff" of learning and, beyond that, of how one sees the whole of reality itself.

RELATION OF OBJECTIVES, LEARNING THEORY, AND PHILOSOPHY

Almost a decade ago, in their book *Psychological Foundations of Education,* Morris Bigge and Maurice Hunt treated the philosophical implications of the two most prominent families of contemporary learning theory: *stimulus-response associationism* and *Gestalt* or *cognitive-field theories.*[11] I recommend that

[10] See especially discussion of the pyramid relationships in Chapter 4, pp. 67–72.

[11] Morris L. Bigge and Maurice P. Hunt, *Psychological Foundations of Education,* pp. 256–370.

the reader carefully examine this in-depth study for himself; he will find Chapters 11, 12, 13, and 14 of particular value. A briefer analysis of these two learning theories which dominate educational thought in this century can be found in *New Strategies and Curriculum in Social Studies* by Frederick Smith and C. Benjamin Cox.[12] Although neither of these works extends its analysis to the kinds of objectives associated with the two major learning families, the present troubled climate of curriculum planning calls for such an extrapolation.

Broadly speaking, *stimulus-response associationism* is compatible with philosophic *positivism* and *realism*.[13] *Gestalt* or *cognitive-field theory* is compatible with philosophic *experimentalism* and, although this point is ignored in Bigge and Hunt's work, also (in my opinion) with the spirit of *existentialism*. I also find that the *behavioral* style of formulating learning objectives is a systemically valid extension of positivism-realism and stimulus-response (or S-R) learning theories. However, experimentalist-existentialist philosophies and Gestalt learning theories support a very different formulation of learning objectives—the *cognitive-affective* variety.

POSITIVISM–REALISM: S–R ASSOCIATIONIST THEORY AND BEHAVIORAL OBJECTIVES

I have identified two broad streams of thought throughout this chapter and the next by the following terms: *positivism-realism—stimulus-response associationist theory* and *experimentalism-existentialism—Gestalt theory*. It is not my inten-

---

[12] Chapter 2, pp. 17–39.

[13] Bigge and Hunt apply stimulus-response associationism primarily to the naturalistic, empirical schools of realism (e.g., B. F. Skinner's operant conditioning), which they find synonymous with philosophic positivism. They caution that whereas stimulus-response associationism does harmonize with some aspects of contemporary classical realism, it does not represent that philosophic position adequately. There are, however, enough parallels between stimulus-response associationism and the classical realism described in Chapter 5 that I will not belabor Bigge and Hunt's distinction.

tion to obliterate the very real differences within these two broad streams of thought. (I refer my reader back to the more detailed philosophic analysis in Chapter 5.) Also, it is not my intention to overlook the possibility of eclecticism on the part of a teacher.[14] However, I believe that the similarities which are the bases of these two *loose* groupings are extremely helpful in understanding the essence of contemporary curriculum conflicts regarding both learning objectives and evaluation procedures.

A significant idea to grasp in distinguishing between the characteristics of the two broad streams of thought is that the total act of learning has an entirely different connotation within each framework. The *stimulus-response* theorist considers that learning takes place when a stimulus is bonded with a response. Thus he is chiefly concerned with helping the student establish desirable S-R bonds. As outlined by Smith and Cox, the stimulus-response theorist assumes

. . . (1) that what is to be learned can be described as small, physical or mental response units ordinarily identified as "answers"; (2) that these response units can be associated in the learner with physical or mental stimulus units—e.g., questions; and (3) that repetition of these associable units coupled with reinforcements such as marks, comments, and grades will tend to fix the desired relationships in the learner.[15]

The above assumptions make good sense to the stimulus-response associationist since he holds a supporting belief characteristic of the positivist-realist world-view—namely, that the universe is a vast mechanism ordered by fixed laws. Moreover, he has incorporated the basic positivist-realist principle of cause and effect—the idea that every event is determined by prior events, and that human thought itself is determined by external stimuli which affect the individual's

[14] See Mehdi Nakosteen's statement on eclecticism quoted in Chapter 4, p. 71.

[15] Frederick R. Smith and C. Benjamin Cox, *New Strategies and Curriculum in Social Studies*, © 1969 by Rand McNally and Company, Chicago, p. 21.

nervous system. In other words, he regards learning as a physiological process:

Learning, even of the simplest kind and in the simplest organisms, is related, of course, to processes in some parts of the nervous system. More complex adaptive behavior depends upon the presence and effective functioning of the cerebral cortex, and different parts of the cortex contribute in different ways to various aspects of learning, remembering, and problem-solving.[16]

Therefore, like the positivist-realist,[17] the stimulus-response associationist is interested in storing within an inherently neutral-passive learner everything that the latter must know in order to adapt properly to his environment:

. . . it appears from psychophysiological evidence that memory has at least two stages: a short-term, quickly fading process during which the experience is initially stored; and a long-term set of mechanisms—involving physical, chemical, and physiological changes—contributing to the storage and availability of learned material over considerable periods of time.[18]

Thus an educator who emphasizes acquisition, recitation, and convergent thinking in his teaching methodology reflects stimulus-response associationism theory:

. . . The statement of one factor—in a teacher's question, for example—is intended to cue the students to express the other factors that they have learned to associate with it. . . . Teachers who ask,

[16] David Krech, Richard S. Crutchfield, and Norman Livson, *Elements of Psychology*, 2nd ed. (New York: Alfred A. Knopf, 1969), p. 15. Copyright © 1969 by Alfred A. Knopf, Inc. I am aware that contemporary behaviorists defend their views as infinitely more complex than classical S-R thought. Nonetheless, there remains a constancy about stimulus-response associationist theories: man—however involved the input-output relationship—is still regarded as "nothing but" *a responsive, biochemical organism.*

[17] Again, the word "realism" in this instance applies primarily to the empirical school, although even the classical realist regards the learner *initially* as a passive receptacle who must be filled with proper "stuff."

[18] Krech, Crutchfield, and Livson, *Elements of Psychology*, p. 15.

"When was the battle of ————— ?" "Who was president when ————— ?" "Where did ————— happen?" are structuring associations in the S-R tradition. Even questions like "Why did ————— occur?" follow the S-R associationism model if the reason or reasons called for were preestablished for the learner.[19]

An examination of behavioral objectives reveals that such objectives (in keeping with stimulus-response associationist theory) are stated from the point of view of the teacher: the specific behavior the teacher wants to elicit, the circumstances surrounding such behavior, and the extent of the behavior desired.[20] The theory underlying behavioral objectives is that the only way to ascertain whether a student has learned a fact, a skill, or a concept is by his *overt* behavior. It is held that an observable behavior pattern can be described for *any* worthwhile learning; consequently, if the student performs the defined behavior, he is said to have achieved the desired learning. Furthermore, because they deal only with what is visible and empirically demonstrable, behavioral objectives are regarded as *quantifiable* in nature—that is, the student's attainment of them can be measured, even if the measurement is only an estimate. An overriding focus on quantification is also the hallmark of the stimulus-response associationist; a typical statement follows:

In order to make a scientific study of the extent and causes of individual differences among man, *we must be able to measure these differences.* . . . although the values we obtain from our measurements are only estimates or approximations of the truth, nevertheless we can state the degree of probability that our estimates are within some specified distance from the truth. [Italics added.][21]

[19] Smith and Cox, *New Strategies and Curriculum*, pp. 25–26.

[20] Cf. formula for behavioral objectives in Earl J. Montague and David P. Butts, "Behavioral Objectives," pp. 33–35. See also the general discussion of behavioral objectives in Robert F. Mager, *Preparing Instructional Objectives*; and *On Writing Behavioral Objectives for English*, ed. John Maxwell and Anthony Tovatt.

[21] Krech, Crutchfield, and Livson, *Elements of Psychology*, p. 16.

What needs to be clearly recognized is that the theory under-girding behavioral objectives matches stimulus-response associationism insofar as the instructional goal focuses on an observable, proposed change in the learner:

A teacher carefully plans which learnings (responses) he wants students to develop. He then induces these responses and associates them with stimuli. . . . [S-R associationists] think of behavior as some kind and degree of measurable muscular or glandular movement. . . . Were adequate devices available, it supposedly could be observed and measured.[22]

One of the teaching methods most obviously rooted in stimulus-response associationism and geared toward the achievement of behavioral objectives is *programmed instruction*. Whether curriculum content is programmed in machines or texts, the format of learning is similar: The subject matter is broken down into isolated bits of information, which are then arranged in a carefully planned series. The assumption is that a learner cannot achieve any understanding of a body of knowledge unless he proceeds as if the knowledge could be studied piecemeal. In the stimulus-response tradition, the whole of something is not ignored, but it is believed to be too big a piece of knowledge for anyone to handle in a learning situation. Consequently, the task is to take a whole, break it down into its component parts, and study each part intensively.[23]

The job of breaking down subject-matter wholes into component parts is precisely the function of the educational programmer. The resulting subject-matter package involves (a) a controlled presentation of the content (for example, the learner is not permitted to go on until he has demonstrated mastery of the given item in the series); (b) action on the learner's part in terms of an overt response; (c) use of cues to elicit the *correct response*; (d) immediate confirmation of the student's success or failure (feedback); and (e) reinforcement

[22] Morris L. Bigge, *Learning Theories for Teachers* (New York: Harper & Row, 1964), pp. 81, 211.

[23] Cf. Krech, Crutchfield, and Livson, *Elements of Psychology*, pp. 5–6.

of correct responses so that the learner is able to proceed independently at his own pace from familiar background to new, previously determined terminal behavior.[24]

From a behavioral point of view, learning objectives stated in such terms as "understandings," "appreciations," and "developments" are vague and utterly useless since such things cannot be observed, and therefore are not measurable guides to instruction.[25] The key to writing functional behavioral objectives is the presumed ability of a teacher to *know* what and when a learner learns. Below are a number of social studies objectives phrased in behavioral terms; they illustrate the prescribed way to formulate objectives. Each has *an observable behavior as its goal* and *a predetermined competency level.* Whether the desired goals concern knowledge, inquiry, or attitudes and values, the objectives reflect a world-view which is limited to externalized stimulus-response matters. They also reflect a knowledge-view which holds, in the pattern of positivist-realist philosophies, that existence and reality are identical. On the premise that "A is A," teachers employing behavioral objectives will assume that students should *converge in thought and action* as they achieve the stated objectives.

BEHAVIORAL KNOWLEDGE OBJECTIVES

Can recall within three minutes the names of nine out of the eleven twentieth-century American presidents.

Can recognize in a timed matching test the correct dates of the administrations of the twentieth-century American presidents.

BEHAVIORAL INQUIRY OBJECTIVES

Can recall analytical questions about the nature of political leadership to apply to new data.

Can recognize from a list of ten facts the five pieces of data which support a given generalization.

[24] For a detailed description of programmed instruction, see *Programmed Instruction: Bold New Venture*, ed. Allen D. Calvin.

[25] See, e.g., the nonbehavioral objectives in the sample plans in Chapter 5, pp. 108, 122, and 131.

BEHAVIORAL OBJECTIVES REGARDING ATTITUDES AND VALUES

Demonstrates by raising his hand or giving other cues in class that he is willing to participate in class discussion.

Defends his opinions with factual evidence rather than with appeals to authority, superstition, or some other similar source.

Indicates that he reflects upon substantive values by examining them in terms of evidence introduced by the teacher in class.[26]

EXPERIMENTALISM–EXISTENTIALISM: GESTALT THEORY AND COGNITIVE–AFFECTIVE OBJECTIVES

For Gestaltists, a focus on behavioral objectives is regarded as an emphasis on insignificant and frequently deceptive manifestations of learning. Some experimentalists, it is true, for certain limited purposes, do work with behavioral objectives. However, they would qualify such usage within the experimentalist conception of meaning—that is, they would regard all formulations of knowledge, including learning objectives, as relative, uncertain, and subject to on-going change.[27] Nonetheless, the experimentalist shares the existentialist's rejection

[26] Edwin Fenton, *The New Social Studies* (New York: Holt, Rinehart and Winston, Inc., 1967), p. 23. It should be noted that behavioral objectivists frequently categorize learning goals into "cognitive" and "affective" domains (see, e.g., C. Benjamin Cox, "Behavior as Objective in Education," pp. 445–447). However, when such categorizations are employed, *behaviorists still insist that general objectives from either the cognitive or affective domain be translated into terms which state specific, observable, and measurable learning outcomes.* Since an aura of privacy tends to surround the affective domain, behaviorists thus far have given limited attention to identifying, observing, and measuring affective behaviors. In any event, behavioral uses of the cognitive-affective domains should not be confused with Gestaltist cognitive-affective objectives discussed in the following section of this chapter.

[27] To grasp why some experimentalists can work with behavioral objectives, at least in a limited sense, see Chapter 5, pp. 114–16. Dewey and Lewenstein, it will be recalled, illustrate the traditional experimentalist concern for arriving at socially determined generalizations toward which the young are then guided. Once established, socially determined generalizations can be expressed as learning goals according to the behavioral objective formula. However, experimentalists like Postman and Weingartner can be expected to reject behavioral objectives as a seduction of the young (see Chapter 5, pp. 116–120).

of the more typically prescriptive, rigid nature of behavioral objectives, holding that the tight parameters required in their formulation reflect a fixed, narrow view about the kind of knowledge which is important. And all Gestaltists share a suspicion of what is actually learned through stimulus-response and what is actually measured in the attainment of behavioral objectives. To them, the student's performance in a stimulus-response framework often reflects little more than meaningless rote recall.

The Gestaltist view of stimulus-response associationism is well illustrated in a story told by John Dewey. Visiting a class one day, Dewey asked the students, "What would you find if you dug a hole in the earth?" His question elicited only silence. Finally, the teacher advised Dewey that he had asked the wrong question. Turning to the class, she queried, "What is the state of the center of the earth?" In unison the class replied, "Igneous fusion."[28]

To gain an understanding of the view of the Gestaltist, one should begin by examining his assumptions regarding learning. The key to the Gestaltist's position is insight, by which he means a sense of, or feeling for, relationships or *a whole pattern*.[29] He considers that learning takes place when an individual gains insight into a problematic situation:

To the extent that the insight accurately interprets the physical environment and is useful in aiding the learner to achieve his goal by helping him to design effective subsequent behavior, the insight may be called right or true.[30]

It can be seen that the Gestaltist's insight has the same function as the experimentalist's hypothesis, and that the learning process is similar to the latter's reflective method of inquiry.[31]

[28] Cited by Edwin Fenton, *Teaching the New Social Studies in Secondary Schools: An Inductive Approach* (New York: Holt, Rinehart and Winston, Inc., 1966), p. 23.

[29] Bigge and Hunt, *Psychological Foundations*, p. 296.

[30] Frederick R. Smith and C. Benjamin Cox, *New Strategies and Curriculum in Social Studies*, © 1969 by Rand McNally and Company, Chicago, pp. 23–24.

[31] See Chapter 3, pp. 47–48, and Chapter 5, pp. 111–12.

In harmony with both the experimentalist and existentialist world-views, the Gestaltist assumes that experience involves more than a mechanistic connection between the individual and the stimuli in his environment. Unlike the stimulus-response theorist, the Gestaltist believes in the existence of an important *internal* dimension of human life. In the experimentalist-existentialist traditions, he assumes that each individual interacts with his environment. And he holds that the person's "overt, physical behavior may or may not reflect this interaction in a way that can be observed directly."[32] What is implied is that reality and knowledge cannot be divorced from the unique perceptions of individual students:

While Gestaltists do in fact recognize that things, conditions, persons, events, or the like do exist or happen quite independently of a given individual, they suppose that the effect of these environmental factors on the individual depends largely on the way he "feels" about them. *Reality in this school of thought is the person's interpretation of that with which he interacts.* [Italics added.][33]

The Gestaltist also brings to his learning theory the experimentalist-existentialist belief in context, thereby rejecting the stimulus-response associationism idea of a piecemeal approach to the world. He describes learning as a purposeful process which takes place within the whole of an individual's psychological reality, or "life space."[34] This means that the learner has to get a feel for the whole picture of something *before* an examination of parts will make any sense to him.

In the experimentalist-existentialist traditions, the Gestaltist educator necessarily gives a wide latitude to divergent thinking in his teaching methods. This divergency is reflected in the nature of his learning objectives. Specifically, the Gestaltist is concerned with two highly interdependent levels of learning: the *cognitive* and *affective* domains. The purpose of cognitive and especially affective objectives is not to codify precisely

[32] Smith and Cox, *New Strategies and Curriculum*, p. 23.
[33] *Ibid.*
[34] Bigge and Hunt, *Psychological Foundations*, pp. 362–70.

what a student is to "get" or "do" in his pursuit of learning. Rather, such objectives are based on the idea that learning is a developmental process—a process that should be designed, not left merely to chance. But whereas cognitive-affective objectives indicate a preplanned teaching design for learning activities, they do so *without prescribing or limiting what may happen to students as they get involved in those activities*. It is this fundamentally different attitude toward the end results of learning activities which sets apart the two schools of thought on the matter of writing objectives. Behavioral objectives strip learning of the element of mystery, while cognitive and affective objectives are stated generally enough to anticipate the unknown. Let us examine the latter more closely.

Cognitive objectives are concerned with informational levels of learning. Typically these are subdivided into two groups:

(1) COGNITIVE KNOWLEDGE OBJECTIVES. These range all the way from concrete to abstract knowledge and from simple to complex behavior. Essentially, they involve the student's ability to recall or recognize ideas or phenomena he has previously experienced. Illustrations of knowledge objectives in the cognitive domain follow:

To define technical terms by giving their attributes, properties, or relations.

The recall of major facts about particular cultures.

Knowledge of criteria for the evaluation of recreational activities.

Knowledge of scientific methods for evaluating health concepts.

Knowledge of the important principles by which our experience with biological phenomena is summarized.

The recall of major theories about particular cultures.

Knowledge of a relatively complete formulation of the theory of evolution.[35]

(2) COGNITIVE INTELLECTUAL ABILITIES AND SKILLS. This order of cognitive objectives involves the student's ability to locate

[35] B. S. Bloom and D. R. Krathwohl, *Taxonomy of Educational Objectives: Handbook I, the Cognitive Domain* (New York: David McKay Company, Inc., 1956), appendix.

information and to utilize techniques in solving problems. Basically, it deals with his ability to use the experimentalist techniques of reflective inquiry. Illustration of cognitive objectives of this type are listed below:

Skill in translating mathematical verbal material into symbolic statements and vice versa.

The ability to grasp the thought of the work as a whole at any desired level of generality.

Skill in predicting continuation of trends.

The ability to predict the probable effect of a change in a factor on a biological situation previously at equilibrium.

The ability to recognize unstated assumptions.

Skill in distinguishing facts from hypotheses.

Ability to check the consistency of hypotheses with given information and assumptions.

Ability to propose ways of testing hypotheses.[36]

As can be observed from the above illustrations, both groups of cognitive objectives focus on factual levels of thinking. However, since the Gestaltist regards facts in the subjective sense of experimentalist-existentialist philosophies, he will expect considerable variation in the ways his students go about relating to cognitive objectives. Phrased another way, cognitive objectives do not describe *the* visible clues or *the* competency levels by which the teacher can determine whether desirable learning has taken place. Although such a teacher surely attempts to achieve empathy with his students, he realizes that he can never get inside the perceptions of another person. Consequently, when he looks for overt clues, he does so cautiously. He neither predetermines the nature of learning clues nor ignores the possibility that individuals will bring radically different interpretations to the factual, or cognitive, domain of knowledge.

The *affective* domain of Gestaltist objectives is viewed as the highest and most important level since it involves the ap-

[36] *Ibid.*

plication of whatever the student learns at the cognitive level. (The reader will discern an affinity between affective objectives and experimentalist-existentialist "generalizations.") Specifically, affective objectives are concerned with the development of attitudes, understandings, appreciations, and values. Several illustrations are listed below:

AFFECTIVE LEARNING OBJECTIVES

Develops awareness of aesthetic factors in dress, furnishings, architecture, city design, good art, and the like.

Appreciation (tolerance) of cultural patterns exhibited by individuals from other groups—religious, social, political, economic, national, etc.

Increase in sensitivity to human need and pressing social problems.

Alertness toward human values and judgments on life as they are recorded in literature.

Enjoyment of self-expression in music and in arts and crafts as another means of personal enrichment.

Continuing desire to develop the ability to speak and write effectively.

Grows in sense of kinship with human beings of all nations.

Devotion to those ideas and ideals which are the foundations of democracy.

Develops a consistent philosophy of life.[37]

Since affective objectives deal with highly subjective feelings, emotions, and values, they do *not* necessarily lend themselves to visible behavior nor to quantifiable measurement. Furthermore, many affective objectives describe long-range behavior and attitude goals; hence immediate and observable feedback on the attainment of such objectives would be regarded as premature, distorted, and unwarranted. Actually, it is impossible for a teacher to judge whether most of the important learnings expressed in affective terms *ever* really

[37] D. R. Krathwohl, B. S. Bloom, and B. B. Masia, *Taxonomy of Educational Objectives: Handbook II, the Affective Domain* (New York: David McKay Company, Inc., 1964), appendix.

transpire. As Roszak has said, a person may be able to express what he knows only by "eloquent silence." But from the experimentalist-existentialist-Gestaltist point of view, the inability of the teacher to provide immediate, tangible, and precise evidence in no way lessens the importance of the affective level of learning. Educators who are comfortable in working toward affective aims simply hold with the social worker Charlotte Towle that insofar as determining the actual results of one's labors, "a profession makes the emotional demand of enduring denial and frustration in *not knowing*." However, the "not knowing" on the part of the teacher (and administrators and the tax-paying public) need not preclude the student *himself* from knowing. And educating man in terms other than a quality-controlled and predetermined "product" need not prevent us from living a qualitative existence made richer by its infinite variety and more exciting by its ultimate mystery.

CHAPTER SEVEN

THE ACHILLES HEEL
OF TEACHING: EVALUATION

The various philosophic orientations undergirding the "stuff" of curriculum shape not only learning objectives but also evaluation methods. Unfortunately, this connection between philosophic assumptions and evaluation procedures is not made by most educators; hence evaluation reflects the same discontinuity found in virtually all other curriculum matters. But the discontinuity at this point—the culminating level of teaching and learning—poses a particularly serious ethical problem: The highly questionable judgments made about the quality of a student's educative experience become a permanent part of his cumulative school record, and that record has a long-range influence on his life.

Despite the importance of evaluation in the lives of students, it represents, for all practical purposes, the Achilles heel of classroom teaching. Given little in-depth thought, evaluation procedures tend to be handled in a perfunctory manner—often governed by what "everyone else" seems to be doing in the school or by what takes the least amount of time. Typically this means for the teacher a chief concern of getting a prescribed (or at least a recommended) number of grades into his grade book prior to the end of a marking period.

In addition to being the most vulnerable spot in the teacher's makeup, evaluation is also the most powerful tool at his disposal. To be both vulnerable and powerful is to stand on dangerous ground. Legions of teachers, for example, feel at a loss in determining fair and reasonable means of assessing student progress—means by which they can feel comfortable in justifying whatever notations they enter as a part of the student's permanent record. To these teachers evaluation is an awkward appendage to the learning activities. Rather than squarely face the discomfort of their tenuous rationale, such teachers tend to withdraw from evaluation concerns. Both to themselves and to their students they are likely to insist that "evaluation is not the really important part of learning anyway." Yet when those same teachers hand out report cards at the end of each marking period, their students know better.

Still other teachers see evaluation as a means of luring students in a given direction and/or as a means of threatening and penalizing them in the face of unwanted behavior. I have observed, for example, the ease with which student teachers consider evaluation procedures a convenient method of handling discipline problems. When they ask me, "Am I too easy with my students? Should I tighten up?" they frequently imply the use of grades as a weapon of classroom control.

Teachers operating from the above-described positions are obviously not looking at evaluation as a component of a totally integrated system of thought. Consistent with the theme of this book, I hold that legitimate evaluation procedures are those which the teacher can explain as conscious derivatives of his basic assumptions concerning the nature of the world, knowledge, and values.

Again let me ask the reader to consider the pyramid construct developed in Chapter 4.[1] Viewed from a philosophically

---

[1] See Chapter 4, pp. 67–72.

systemic frame of reference, evaluation is simply an extension of axiological, or value-view ideas. Therefore, unless we would continue the pretext that evaluation is handled in a uniform way by all teachers and that the student's cumulative record tells him something about his ability and worth which he ought never to question seriously, it seems imperative that teachers communicate their positions to their students. In short, students have a right to know why their various teachers do not use the same evaluation rules. For example, they need to realize that if a teacher conceives of reality and knowledge in the positivist-realist tradition and has formulated his learning objectives in behavioral terms, then his evaluation practices may well be based on precise measurements—a perfectly logical, justifiable procedure *within that framework*. On the other hand, students need to recognize that a teacher who functions from the experimentalist-existentialist-Gestaltist tradition may use much more subjective evaluation techniques, which can be fully justified within that tradition.

As the reader works through his own evaluation rationale against his underlying philosophic ideas, it will be helpful for him to consider the most glaring assessment problems: academic standards, the normal curve, mistake-making, and grades. These four interrelated factors often assume the same deceptive neutrality which Theodore Roszak attributes to the technocratic mentality.[2] That is, because certain rules based on these four factors prevail throughout the educational system, we concentrate not on these regulations but on what happens to individuals as they operate within them. We tend to ignore the unobtrusive umpire figures who stand above the contest and judge the contenders.

ACADEMIC STANDARDS

For example, the notion that achievement ought to be interpreted in terms of established *academic standards* is almost sacrosanct. In the post-Sputnik era, the great outpouring of

[2] See Roszak quotation in Chapter 6, pp. 139–40.

rhetoric over "maintaining high standards in our schools" has indicated the role which this notion plays in the thinking of both American educators and their lay critics. Actually, the obsession with standards is understandable if one sees that evaluation cannot be accomplished in a vacuum. The process necessitates some kind of criteria against which the teacher can make certain judgments. But the crux of the matter (and this tends to be ignored in arguments over the "raising" or "lowering" of educational standards) is that *the criteria used to give meaning to standards are not neutral.*

Perhaps the most fundamental question which a teacher needs to ponder before he resolves the issue of standards to his own satisfaction is whether *quantification* of achievement is compatible with his knowledge-view and learning theory. As pointed out in the discussion of behavioral and cognitive-affective objectives in the previous chapter, a quantification of what is learned is irrelevant or of minimal concern within the experimentalist and the existentialist orientations but makes good sense within the positivist and the realist orientations.

THE NORMAL CURVE

A popular quantification method of judging the performance of students is, of course, the *normal curve*. In fact, many teachers regard the curve as the fairest, most efficient way of maintaining high academic standards. Because of the longtime prestige which the normal curve enjoys, its difficulties are worth examining closely.

No two classes are ever quite alike in terms of student performance. Nonetheless, grades which are derived from a standardized mathematical norm of achievement do tend to fall into a curve, the shape of which is determined by the performance of the individuals within the class. Although it is possible that the grades will fall into a "normal," bell-shaped curve, it is just as possible that the curve will be askew one way or the other. What must be kept in mind is that the normal curve is essentially a mathematical ideal, not in the sense of a standard of perfection but in the sense of a product of the imagination—a device used as a basis for comparison and for fostering competition. No universal law governs the form that frequency distributions of grades of students in general take, but in the usual class of thirty to thirty-five students, the number of students is *much too small* to expect results to approximate a normal curve. However, if a reasonably large number of measures of some trait are tabulated (for example, the scores of a standardized objective test administered to five classes of senior high school algebra students), the scores often will approximate a normal frequency distribution.

The "ideal" percents of distribution on a normal curve have been established in terms of fixed distance from the mean or the average student score: 7, 24, 38, 24, and 7 percent. This serves as a convenient statistical basis for determining the percentages of students who are subsequently evaluated as having done A, B, C, D, or F work. It also explains why many classroom teachers automatically expect that the majority of their students will earn B's, C's, and D's and that the much smaller number of A's will be offset by about the same number of F's. The extent to which the normal curve has engraved itself on educational thinking is illustrated by the number of teachers who judge their own test constructions to be good or bad in terms of whether the resulting student scores fall into a normal curve distribution.

Probably the most destructive aspect of the normal curve method of assessing student performance is its encouragement of a self-fulfilling prophecy. The following comment is by Benjamin Bloom, one of the foremost scholars in educational evaluation:

Each teacher begins a new term (or course) with the expectation that about a third of his students will adequately learn what he has to teach. He expects about a third of his students to fail or to just "get by." Finally, he expects another third to learn a good deal of what he has to teach, but not enough to be regarded as "good students." This set of expectations, supported by school policies and practices in grading, becomes transmitted to the students through the grading procedures and through the methods and materials of instruction. The system creates a self-fulfilling prophecy such that the final sorting of students through the grading process becomes approximately equivalent to the original expectations.[3]

Bloom has pointed out further that the normal curve, because of its application within highly fluctuating educational circumstances, actually contradicts the idea of established academic standards. If he is correct in his analysis, the only thing the normal curve distribution seems to tell us is that a teacher is doing an extremely poor job of educating:

We have for so long used the normal curve in grading students that we have come to believe in it. Our achievement measures are designed to detect differences among our learners, even if the differences are trivial in terms of the subject matter. We then distribute our grades in a normal fashion. In any group of students we expect to have some small percent receive A grades. We are surprised when the percentage differs greatly from about 10 percent. We are also prepared to fail an equal proportion of students. Quite frequently this failure is determined by the rank order of the students in the group rather than by their failure to grasp the essential ideas of the course. Thus, we have become accustomed to classify students into about five categories of level of performance and to assign grades in some relative fashion. *It matters not that the failures of one year performed at about the same level as the C students of another year. Nor does it matter that the A students of one school do about as well as the F students of another school.*

Having become "conditioned' to the normal distribution, we set grade policies in these terms and are horrified when some teacher attempts to recommend a very different distribution of grades. Administrators are constantly on the alert to control teachers who are "too easy" or "too hard" in their grading. A teacher whose grade distribution is normal will avoid difficulties with administrators. But even more important, we find ways of convincing students that they can only do C work or D work by our grading system and even by our system of quiz and progress testing.

[3] Benjamin S. Bloom, "Learning for Mastery," *UCLA Evaluation Comment* (May, 1968), p. 1.

Finally, we proceed in our teaching as though only the minority of our students should be able to learn what we have to teach.

There is nothing sacred about the normal curve. It is the distribution most appropriate to chance and random activity. Education is a purposeful activity and we seek to have the students learn what we have to teach. If we are effective in our instruction, the distribution of achievement should be very different from the normal curve. In fact, we may even insist that our education efforts have been unsuccessful to the extent to which our distribution of achievement approximates the normal distribution. [Italics added.][4]

Bloom's conclusion that most students ("perhaps over 90 percent") could achieve high-level success in the learning process is, of course, revolutionary in its implications. But one cannot help speculating about the approximately 10 percent safety factor of success that Bloom affords himself. This statistical safety factor seems likely to sanction the traditional policy of anticipating the failure or limited success of *some* students even if the percentage is much smaller than in prevailing practices.

John Holt, among others, has provided us with some fresh insights into the mysteries of intelligence and the amazing ability of even *severely retarded teen-agers* to do intellectual work of very high quality. After describing the remarkable mathematical work accomplished by one retarded boy in a forty-minute demonstration conducted by Caleb Gattegno, a professor of mathematics and psychology, Holt concluded:

It is the tragedy of his life that he will probably never again find himself with a man like Gattegno, who knows, as few teachers do, that it is his business to put himself into contact with the intelligence of his students, wherever and whatever that may be, and who has enough intuition and imagination to do it. He has not done much work with retarded children, but he saw in a moment what I might have taken days or weeks to find out, or might never have found out: that to get in touch with the intelligence of these children, to give them solid ground to stand and move on, he had to go way, way back, to the very beginning of learning and under-

[4] *Ibid.*, pp. 2–3.

standing. Nor was this all he brought to the session. Equally important was a kind of respect for these children, a conviction that under the right circumstances they could and would do first-class thinking. There was no condescension or pity in his manner, nor even any noticeable sympathy. For the duration of the class he and these children were no less than colleagues, trying to work out a tough problem—and working it out.[5]

Surely the retarded boy in Holt's illustration would be among those deemed incapable of achieving success in conventional school learning environments—even under Bloom's vastly liberalized statistical projection. It seems to me that the educational implications of Gattegno's demonstration class are staggering for teachers assigned to teach heterogeneous but relatively normal youth, whether in our urban slums or affluent suburbia. What is strongly suggested is the need for a probing analysis of the meanings of human intelligence within the framework of virtually *all* educational philosophies, including those which rely heavily on measurement devices. Gattegno's experiences, in my opinion, dramatically expose the normal curve set of expectations for what it is— a lethal teaching mentality which conceals the real potentialities of human intelligence.

MISTAKE-MAKING

Another fundamental matter which the teacher needs to consider carefully in coming to grips with the issues of standards, the normal curve, and grades, is how he regards *mistake-making*. Most educators seem to view academic error the way that a moralist views sin. American students are con-

---

[5] From the book *How Children Fail* by John Holt. Copyright © 1964 by Pitman Publishing Corporation, p. 95. Reprinted by permission of Pitman Publishing Corp. For supporting descriptions of the remarkable learning capacities of severely brain-damaged children, see Joan Beck, "Unlocking the Secrets of the Brain." For another account of the powerful influence of teacher attitudes and teacher expectations on the performance of students, see Robert Rosenthal and Lenore Jacobson, *Pygmalion in the Classroom.*

fronted with curricula that are overwhelmingly mistake-centered, with their "achievement" largely determined on the basis of how many mistakes they have managed to avoid. Yet I would remind the reader of the implications of speculative-intuitive science as discussed in Chapter 3.[6] Within that framework of thinking, mistake-making is not something to be avoided; it is a vital aspect of learning. And rather than penalizing a student for departing from a preexisting standard and grading him in the light of his "failure" to meet a desired level of performance, a teacher oriented to speculative-intuitive thinking would encourage intellectual risk-taking and leaps into the unknown.

GRADES

Many educators, of course, equate evaluation with *grades*. For them, the entire assessment process is a matter of simple arithmetic. They carefully record the digital scores and/or letter grades which they have awarded to each student during a prescribed period of time. Then they add these up, divide by the appropriate figure, perhaps relate their findings to some statistical curve, and finally arrive at a symbolic representation of the student's accomplishments.

In my opinion, the practice of culminating a course by reducing the success of each student to a single, all-encompassing letter grade cannot be supported in any public school within a pluralistic society. The practice is, in fact, a symptom of the narcissistic attitude described in an earlier chapter: a final grade functions as a club to enforce student conformity to a particular point of view. Unfortunately, it serves this purpose *whether or not the teacher desires it to have such an effect*. I believe this is true regardless of the way in which a final letter grade is calculated.

Some teachers seek to get around the difficulties inherent in the normal curve by grading their students according to one of the *fixed criteria* methods—the *uniform point system*,

[6] See pp. 58–63.

for example. In this method the teacher compiles a series of measurements of his students' mastery of predetermined information or skills. For example, if a student earns 425 points out of a possible 500, he might be guaranteed a final grade of B.

Another fixed criteria method of evaluation is the *contract system*, in which each student is guaranteed a specified grade upon his completion of certain predetermined tasks. The teacher is not at all concerned with comparing the performance levels of his students; instead, he focuses his attention on the task-completion level of the individual student and evaluates him according to the terms of the learning contract. Under the contract system it is quite conceivable that all students in a class will earn the same final letter grade. In fact, for all students to be motivated enough to complete the maximum terms of a contract would be regarded as an indication of teaching and learning success.

Teachers who use the contract system point out that mediocrity of work (or lowered standards) is not a necessary corollary of this evaluation system. It need not pose a "quantity versus quality" choice since a teacher can be as rigorous or flexible about quality as he desires to be. The mere turning in of work need not be regarded as fulfillment of the learning contract. The teacher can return any student work which does not meet his criteria for satisfactory scholarship, with the request that it be redone and resubmitted. He can hold all his students to an identical standard of "satisfactory scholarship," or he can consider highly varying factors in the lives of individual students as he assesses what constitutes acceptable completion of the learning tasks.

But even when a teacher employs a uniform point system or a contract system of evaluation, *he cannot avoid the factor of teacher bias*. His criteria still will reflect his own point of view—whatever it represents and however firm or flexible it might be. Fixed criteria do have definite appeal for educators who want to get away from a competitive grading atmosphere, and this, in my opinion, is no small advantage. The use of competition in the education of our youth is a highly controversial matter. Pressure for making our public schools competitive arenas comes from those persons who see reality and human nature as a Social Darwinist "survival of the fittest" struggle.[7] Proponents often equate academic competition with the health of the free enterprise system, and they regard all attempts to minimize competition in schools as subversive threats to the well-being of the nation. My own view is deeply colored by the many researchers who have emphasized the negative effects of competition upon individuals who must live in an increasingly interdependent society. I am convinced that pitting student against student serves to motivate only those individuals who are experiencing school success. Those who have had repeated failures find competition a frustrating experience and tend to withdraw.[8] In the last analysis, however, I would emphasize that final grades calculated on the basis of a contract or cumulative point system are no more neutral than grades derived from normal curve percentages.

The above problems are not introduced here for the purpose of categorically condemning the use of academic standards, the normal curve, and grades. Consistent with my own educational philosophy and view of the good, the true, and the beautiful, I personally reject arguments which support any kind of grading system. Within the boundaries of my own classroom situation, my preference is to write comments on student work instead of assigning grades—whether on examination papers, essays, term papers, or other projects. By raising additional questions, posing alternative points of view, frequently playing the role of the devil's advocate, the written-comment technique (in contrast with terminal digital scores or letter grades) tends to provoke further response

[7] See, e.g., Giles F. Liegerot, "Is Academic Competition for You?", pp. 148–52. See also the discussion of Social Darwinism as a part of the American ideological core in Chapter 2, p. 35.

[8] Cf. Arthur W. Combs, "The Myth of Competition," pp. 264–69; Henry A. Davidson, "Competition, the Cradle of Anxiety," pp. 162–66; and Henry A. Davidson, Merritt L. Schriver, and Herman J. Peters, "Should Johnny Compete or Cooperate?" pp. 30–32.

from students. In this way I am able to utilize the work of students to promote on-going dialogue with them.

Nonetheless, I am fully committed to the concept of pluralism in teaching as in all other aspects of our culture. Hence I respect the fact that some educators do regard knowledge in terms of a fixed body of ideas and established standards of achievement, and also the fact that some look upon grades as external motivating devices.[9] Therefore, although I am not at all sympathetic with the practice of putting digital scores or letter grades on student work, I support the right of other educators to do so. Accordingly, if a teacher chooses to see himself as an exemplar of certain necessary ideas and behavior, or as a transmitter of an essential body of knowledge, or as the possessor of certain desirable skills, and if he wishes to measure his students in terms of their proximity to his particular way of thinking and behaving, I would voice no objection to his grading of tests and other activities *if he uses the results only in communicating with the individual student.* That is, I support the teacher's right to advise a student that he has earned a certain grade arrived at on the basis of that teacher's philosophy and corresponding criteria of success. But I strenuously object to the official reporting of such grades *beyond* the classroom situation. To enforce uniform academic standards on a district- or school-wide basis and to use grades or digital scores for any purpose other than private teacher-student communication is to deny the student the ultimate freedom to choose *his* own attitude and *his* own way in any given set of circumstances. Stated another way, the practice of assigning final grades shifts the focus of education away from meaningful personal learning to mere conformity for the sake of survival.

The key point at issue here—that of making final grades a part of each student's permanent, official record of educational achievement (a record, remember, that will follow him for the rest of his life)—is *highly reductionist.* Officially reported final grades are treated as if they had resulted from

[9] Notably educators operating within positivist-realist philosophies and stimulus-response learning theories.

a common pool of basic assumptions, as if all teachers across the nation had arrived at their A's, B's, C's, D's, and F's from the same base. Grades recorded on a student's transcript are subsequently regarded as the official monetary exchange of education, and the hallowed grade-point average is seen as the student's academic net worth—a qualitative assessment which is supposed to be uniformly interpreted by all teachers and all educational institutions.

Sometimes a comparison is made between educational grading practices and the value of a dollar. Despite regional variations in purchasing power, a dollar bill has a fairly uniform value across the nation. When one refers to a unit of the dollar (for example, fifty cents), one can assume that other persons will assign the same general value, or meaning, to it. The uniformity of value of units in a monetary system is derived, of course, from the common standard of exchange, whether that standard is gold, silver, credit, or a combination thereof. However, to regard student grades as having uniform value like money, to treat them as if they are derived from a common standard of exchange, is absurd. The pluralistic values held by educators, reflecting the diverse composition of American society as a whole, make it impossible to calculate grades according to a common standard of exchange. Thus the policy of using official transcripts which require teachers to reduce student achievement to grades perpetuates a bogus evaluation standard. In truth, the official transcripts of student grades used throughout the educational system are unintelligible.[10]

Furthermore, the practice of recording final grades cannot be defended even by those educators who regard a competitive learning atmosphere as endemic to the American way of life. Competition, in the American spirit of fair play and "May the best man win," accords to all competitors equal opportunities for victory. But the issuing of final grades by ideologically diverse teaching personnel is akin to forcing

[10] Cf. Robert L. Shannon, "The Numbers Racket in Education," in *The New Idea in Education*, eds. J. A. Battle and Robert L. Shannon, pp. 76–79.

students to run a series of races in which they leave from different starting gates, race over different tracks, head toward different destinations, and contend with different weather conditions. Consequently, there is no fair basis on which to judge their racing records (grade-point averages).

Unfortunately, official grading procedures are frequently defended on the basis of teaching and administrative convenience. To assume that students cannot progress through our schools on any basis other than a spurious grading system is to underestimate human ingenuity and intelligence. I am convinced that if several million American educators were *aware* of the profound implications of their present practices, and if their enormous pool of talents were stirred, some truly humane and equitable evaluation procedures could be developed.

AN ALTERNATIVE PROCEDURE

Lest I be accused of opening a painful wound and doing nothing more, I would like to suggest one alternative procedure for finally evaluating any course of study. My recommendation involves the elimination of final recorded grades and the substitution of two official recording procedures.

First, I recommend adoption of a simple Pass designation on official student records if all the required work of a course has been completed. The criteria for "required work" would be established by each classroom teacher. My preference for a simple Pass designation rather than Pass-Fail is based on several considerations: The Pass designation actually provides all the information necessary for administrative purposes; that is, it indicates that a student has met the requirements of a particular course and therefore can proceed with his program of studies. If a student does not meet the requirements of a course, the absence of both the course title and a Pass designation on his official record is sufficient indication of the status of his study program. The recording of a Fail designation serves *no positive learning function*. Instead, it sets up roadblocks to engendering students' interest in trying again (perhaps with *different* teachers) and in continuing to learn at their own pace. Despite the lip service that educators give to "individualizing" learning, prevailing expectations of student failure completely ignore the possibility that all students can attain success in a learning task *if they are given enough time*.[11]

Second, I recommend that a written statement describing the growth of a student be made a part of his official record at the *succcessful* culmination of a course, with no statement to be entered on the record if the course is not successfully completed. This procedure already has a precedent in the teacher-parent conference sheets used in some school systems. However, a problem often arises in the triteness and repetitious nature of the comments made on such sheets. In the critical matter of officially evaluating other human lives, it seems to me that teachers have an ethical obligation to develop their observation skills and reporting abilities. These will be immeasurably enhanced if teachers deliberately work at an extremely important teaching technique—*listening to students and listening to the parents of students*. Let me caution the reader that many students blend into indistinguishable blobs in the thinking of a teacher because of his preoccupation with the sound of his own voice. The evaluation of an "indistinguishable blob" will not lend itself to the kind of descriptive reporting I am advocating here.

In answer to the inevitable questions which will be raised concerning feasible methods of reporting a student's progress to his parents, to other teachers, and to the universities, Ernest Melby has written:

My answer is let us be both informative and conducive to the growth of the pupil's self-concept. Let us describe his growth in meaningful terms that are really descriptive of the pupil's effort, unique qualities, interests, attitudes, and behaviors. As for standards, we would evaluate each pupil in terms of his own capacity and growth, not in comparison with others who are very different. . . . As for university entrance, from four years of high school

[11] Cf. John B. Carroll, "A Model of School Learning," pp. 723–33.

experience we should be able to decide what kind of post-high school education the student should undertake. We either recommend him to the state university or the junior college. You say on what basis? When you go to the doctor for a history and physical check-up, the doctor writes constantly as you talk describing your condition. He accumulates for you a medical history. He does not give you an "A" or "B." He does not use meaningless terms which blot out your individuality.[12]

By accumulating the student's educational history—through noting significant observations on the student throughout a course—the classroom teacher would have a definite basis for writing a final descriptive analysis of (1) what seemed to be the student's situation at the start of the course, (2) what seemed to be his situation at the end, and (3) his prognosis. Since a descriptive analysis implies a highly individualized report, no stereotyped format can be offered. Nor can a stereotyped formula for growth itself be offered. Because of differences in philosophic orientations and learning objectives, some teachers will be much more concerned with evaluating *emotional* and *social growth* than *academic growth*. Others will be interested in assessing growth in various areas. Nonetheless, the reader might find some guidelines in this sample descriptive analysis, which focuses primarily on academic growth:

A major objective of the English 302 class was the development of the students' abilities to interpret and appreciate selected works from Western literature. Generally the students were asked to read a particular work. Following each reading, their ideas were shared in small groups and full-class discussions, and then each student was asked to write an essay expressing his own interpretation and evaluation of the work. Mary did not begin this class against a background of extensive readings, nor with a very positive attitude toward books. During the first half of the semester she participated in class discussions only on a minimum basis. However, contact with the ideas expressed by other students seemed to spark her

[12] Ernest O. Melby, *The Deprived Child: His Gift to Education* (East Lansing, Mich.: Mott Institute for Community Improvement, Michigan State University, June, 1966).

interest in reading. Her written compositions were well done from the start, and she showed early skill in going beyond the mundane fact to the interrelationships among ideas. After I read a number of her papers to the rest of the class as examples of good interpretive thinking, I noted that Mary's oral participation sharply increased. By the end of the semester she was one of the outstanding spokesmen of the class. Her new habit of referring her fellow students to other readings—beyond those required as a basis for the course—would seem to indicate that she is developing a genuine appreciation for literature.

Some teachers are likely to interpret Mary's visible behavior much more subjectively and to surround their conclusions about her "success" with a qualifying attitude. For example, one might expect experimentalist-existentialist educators to describe their assessments more in such terms as, "It *might* be thus and so. . . ." or "I have no way of really knowing what Mary is feeling about this, but it is possible. . . ." or "It may be that I am reading my own bias into Mary's behavior, but it seems to me. . . ."[13]

I do not wish to minimize the difficulties involved in any evaluation procedure, including the above recommendations. I recognize that it would be quite possible for a teacher to accord the Pass status only to a small percentage of his students, and that it would be equally possible for a teacher to write so-called "success" descriptions of his students that would be as damaging to them as the F stigma. But despite the ever-present risks, I believe that my recommendations embody two important advantages beyond those already mentioned: First, a descriptive analysis would give some indication of the nature, content, purpose, and methodology of the *course*, itself, in addition to providing the teacher's assessment of a student's success therein. Unlike the undecipherable letter-grade system (in which the course remains an enigma),

[13] For an appreciation of the reluctance of some educators to draw conclusions as firmly as those stated in the above illustration, I refer the reader back to the Roszak passage in Chapter 6, p. 137, wherein he suggests that what a person knows he "may only be able to express by eloquent silence."

the descriptive analysis would give future reviewers of a student's official academic record a broader-based opportunity to make their own assessments of the quality of the student's educational experiences. In other words, a descriptive commentary would communicate to others as much about the teacher and the substance of the course as it would about the student. Second, I believe that the deliberate removal of an official Fail option (and variations thereof) would encourage teachers to rechannel their energies toward providing success experiences for all their students. In effect, teachers would not be *invited* to fail their students.

Since the majority of our schools currently regard student evaluation as a phenomenon which culminates with the official recording of final grades, the reader is likely to find the above recommendations quite removed from the realities of the teaching situation in which he finds himself. He is also likely to be overwhelmed by the volume of work involved in the descriptive approach to evaluation. Admittedly, for teachers to assume the task of maintaining on-going, descriptive records and of writing in-depth, individualized final evaluations on students in lieu of grades would require a serious reappraisal of current teaching loads. (Secondary teachers, for example, typically are responsible for about 150 students.) But to maintain the present teacher-pupil ratio on the grounds of administrative necessity, and to sanction the grading policies which such a ratio fosters, is devastating in human terms.[14] Moreover, the old argument that we do not have sufficient teaching personnel to staff our schools no longer holds. The much-advertised glut of educators on today's job market *could* be tapped to humanize the operation of our schools.

I believe that any teacher, if he so desires, can incorporate individualized descriptive evaluations into his teaching situation, even if official policy still demands a final letter grade. If the reader has serious reservations about altering the evalua-

[14] See, e.g., Harold Addington, "The 1.97–2.00 Syndrome," pp. 6–7.

tion status quo because of the time factor and present heavy teaching loads, he might examine the amount of time many teachers now spend correcting stacks of written quizzes and evaluating the "Friday examination." Whereas I urge a drastic lowering of the teacher-pupil ratio in our schools, I also suggest a critical reappraisal of the present use of teachers' time.

It is an understatement to say that our prevailing reductionist methods of evaluation demand earnest questioning. However, such questions must first be raised by individual educators. Similarly, grading procedures will not be changed unless teachers themselves initiate such change. The fact is that in this matter of evaluation American educators as a whole are caught in a web of contradiction, inconsistency, and confusion. It is hoped that the new generation of teachers will help to untangle the web and accept the responsibilities of living without professional consensus on evaluation as they must learn to live without professional consensus in their underlying philosophies.

Part Three
A Philosophical Outlook

CHAPTER EIGHT

A COMMON DENOMINATOR

A former public school superintendent recently offered his solution for renovating the schools: "Teachers must stand before kids as whole men who know who they are. . . . If we had [such teachers] in abundance, they would change the whole structure, because you can't improve curriculum until you get teachers stimulated and excited, and that doesn't happen until they become deeply involved in what and why they're teaching."[1]

I doubt that anyone would take serious issue with this pronouncement. But unfortunately the "whole" teacher is usually confused with the mythical "ideal" teacher. Somewhere along the line the idea has taken root that there is a theoretical model of a good teacher. This model presumably varies considerably, but nonetheless it embodies certain characteristics which serve as a beacon light, guiding teachers toward appropriate behavior.

[1] From "The Task Is to Learn What Learning Is For," by Bayard Hooper, *Life* Magazine, May 16, 1969, © 1969 Time Inc., p. 39.

THE MYTH OF THE IDEAL TEACHER

The myth of the ideal teacher probably begins during professional preparation itself, when teacher "trainees" ask for and
often receive pat answers to the question, What should I do
as a teacher in this situation? Thereafter the myth is reinforced
by the nation's public schools through their traditional
expectation that faculty will teach particular subjects in much
the same way. Standardization of teaching is encouraged by
the school policy of specifying that certain curriculum content
be "covered" in each class, by the practice of comparing the
achievement-test scores of students taught by different teachers, and by the practice of evaluating teachers themselves on
the basis of a common set of expectations regarding performance and production.

Due to the prevalent belief in the existence of an ideal
teacher—an assumption which does lend itself to a kind of
teaching efficiency and administrative expediency—many persons associated with our schools have

. . . fallen into the trap of specifying quality of instruction in terms
of good and poor teachers, teaching, instructional materials, curriculum—all in terms of group results. We persist in asking such
questions as: What is the best teacher for the group? What is the
best method of instruction for the group? What is the best in-
instructional material for the group?[2]

However, as Benjamin Bloom has emphasized, it is quite possible to start with the opposite assumption that different students may need different kinds of instruction to achieve success in learning. This, of course, is tantamount to saying that
individual students may need *different kinds of teachers*—a
theory which if accepted would reverse efforts to parade educators toward a model teacher.

Although this notion may appear chaotic in its implications,
I propose that it will plunge neither teacher education ,nor
public school programs into a state of unholy disorder. Let me
remind the reader that consonance and dissonance are both

[2] Benjamin S. Bloom, "Learning for Mastery," *UCLA Evaluation Comment* (May, 1968), p. 4.

essential ingredients of harmony. Just as it takes many instruments to make a good orchestra, it takes a highly varied teaching staff to make a good, vital, and stimulating learning environment. To reemphasize the central theme of this book, teachers should be encouraged to develop their own styles in their own ways. This means the deliberate avoidance of professional stereotyping of any kind—by those who are preparing to teach, by those who are teaching teachers to teach, and by those who are hiring, supervising, and evaluating classroom teachers. In short, excellence in teaching—like excellence in learning and in living—is not a uniform phenomenon.

If this posture seems to threaten the continuing existence of American education as an organized system, let me comfort the reader by calling his attention to a powerful idea which could unify a truly pluralistic society. Dietrich Bonhoeffer expressed this idea in his identification of "the fully grown person":

The common denominator must be sought both in thought and in a personal and integrated attitude to life. The man who allows himself to be torn into fragments by events and by questions has not passed the test for the present and the future. . . . *We can never achieve this "wholeness" simply by ourselves, but only together with others.* [Italics added.][3]

Bonhoeffer, of course, was emphasizing our mutual need for one another in the process of finding our individual selves, this need serving as a cohesive social force which grows out of *a mutuality of caring.* However, Bonhoeffer's reference to "others" raises another fundamental question for the educator: Who *are* the "others" who will help him to integrate his individual self? David Riesman has insisted that most contemporary Americans sensitize themselves to the desires and expectations of other persons and then conform to those external directives.[4] His other-directed person is a shallow crea-

---

[3] Dietrich Bonhoeffer, *Letters and Papers from Prison,* p. 108.

[4] David Riesman, Nathan Glazer, and Reuel Denney, *The Lonely Crowd,* pp. 37–38.

ture whose inner fears and insecurities consign him to a psychologically alienated existence—the antithesis of Bonhoeffer's integrated person who finds himself in genuine relationships with other selves.

Teachers, unfortunately, are caught up in shallow, other-directed behavior no less than most persons within our society. Student teachers, for example, often are encouraged to imitate their own teachers, a tendency reflected in a comment made to me by a high school mathematics teacher:

> I remember one thing that my college adviser told me once that I felt was detrimental to teacher preparation. I asked him why there were not more mathematics methods courses, and his reply was: "By the time you have come through sixteen years of school, you will teach as you were taught." To me this is just dittoing mistakes already made![5]

Imitative teaching (actually a blind-following-the-blind attitude) not only perpetuates mistakes but poses a definite obstacle between the teacher and *himself*. In a word, it prevents the teacher from practicing his profession with personal authenticity:

> A person is either himself or not himself; is either rooted in his existence, or a fabrication; has either found his humanhood or is still playing with masks and roles and status symbols. And nobody is more aware of this difference (although unconsciously) than a child. Only an authentic person can evoke a good response in the core of the other person; only person is resonant to person.
>
> Knowledge is not enough. Technique is not enough. Mere experience is not enough. This is the mystery at the heart of the teaching process; and the same mystery is at the heart of the healing process. Both are an art, more than a science or a skill—and the art is at bottom the ability to "tune in to the other's wavelength."
>
> And this ability is not possessed by those who have failed to come to terms with their own individuated person, no matter what other talents they possess. Until they have liberated themselves (not

---

[5] Quoted from a paper written by John Crouse for a graduate course in education, University of Colorado, August, 1969.

completely, but mostly) from what is artificial and unauthentic within themselves, they cannot communicate with, counsel, or control others.

The few teachers who meant the most to me in my school life were not necessarily those who knew the most, but those who gave out the fullness of themselves; who confronted me face to face, as it were, with a humanhood that awoke and lured my own small and trembling soul and called me to take hold of my own existence with my two hands.[6]

THE CULT OF SELF-RIGHTEOUSNESS

It is quite possible that the multiple, nondogmatic, and personally authentic criteria for teaching and learning which I have promoted throughout this work will seem untenable to the reader. In the event that he stands with the growing chorus of voices in contemporary society which insist that we live in a harshly competitive world where deliberate choices must be made *for* individuals in such profound matters as who shall be educated and who shall not be educated, who shall teach and who shall not teach, who shall be heard and who shall not be heard, and even who shall live and who shall not live, then so be it.

But if such is the reader's conviction, let me ask him to rigorously examine his rationale *without automatically assuming that he is a member of the elect.* The person who believes that the elect must prescribe the way in which human lives are to be shaped seldom places himself or his own children in the majority group to be manipulated. The individual who argues that the "fittest" among mankind must prevail rarely places himself beyond the pale of survival. And although such an individual is prone to distrust the competencies of others, he rarely questions his own. In many respects, the self-righteousness which dominates the thinking of many educational and other social reform movements of our day is simply an extension of the exclusive attitude which has fanned the fires

[6] Sidney J. Harris, "Authentic Teachers," *Chicago Daily News* (February 4, 1964).

of violence and destruction throughout the entire human story. Always the self-righteous thinker promulgates a set of givens, and always he negates choice for anyone save himself. His biggest battle is against competing self-righteous thinkers and against opposing sets of givens. Before the reader rushes on the educational scene with a plan to impose his own convictions on other persons, I suggest that he first struggle with his inner self and his own destiny.

A UNIFYING CRITERION

Not long ago I was sitting in my office listening to a middle-aged child psychologist criticize philosophers of education. "You know," he said, "philosophers have been asking the wrong questions for so long they don't begin to realize how far from the marketplace of ideas they are!" When prodded for an elaboration, he went on to point out that the vast majority of people—whatever their level of educational achievement and whatever their occupational focus—could not care less about such speculative inquiry as the nature of the world, knowledge, and values. "Even the professional psychologist, like myself," he insisted, "could give a damn about the fundamental qualities of something called 'knowledge.' He's much more interested in figuring out what makes a biochemical organism respond to an electrode stimulus!" I asked him if he could recommend questions for philosophic inquiry that would be closer to the "marketplace." "Well," he suggested, "why don't the philosophers start giving some prime attention to the most important guts-level question of all: *What is love?*"

As I listened to the child psychologist I couldn't help thinking about an analogy made by Hans Flexner years before. Professor Flexner liked to jolt his graduate students at the University of Denver by comparing people with icebergs. "Most of us," he insisted, "go through life never exposing anything but the mere top of our iceberg—either to ourselves or to other people. Consequently, we spend a lifetime in fruitless, superficial communication with other human beings because we never examine the underlying ideas which cause us to think and act the way we do. In fact, most of us aren't even aware that the hidden part of the iceberg exists!" And so, I thought, even the child psychologist did not seem to be aware that his interest in "figuring out what makes a biochemical organism respond to an electrode stimulus" was colored by his own hidden cluster of assumptions about the nature of man, reality, knowledge, and values.

Nonetheless, I believe that the child psychologist's criticisms did hit upon a key problem. Not that philosophers have been asking the wrong questions; they have simply not pushed the implications of the *right questions* into the marketplace where human lives must be lived. That the question of love was seen by one highly educated critic as beyond the realm of philosophic concerns is illustrative of the popular misconception about the function of philosophy. A serious opinion about the nature and quality of love, of course, requires the most profound kind of value judgment.

I must agree with this critic in the sense that the question of love has been largely ignored in most formal philosophic discourse—and certainly in philosophic discourse which has focused upon educational goals, purposes, content, and methods. Sustained efforts to help either teachers or students see the totality of their individual "icebergs" are extremely rare. Virtually nonexistent are sustained educational efforts to help individuals realize the totality of themselves *in relationship to the totality of other people's beliefs about the world, knowledge, and values.*

All "loving" human relationships, except those that are exploitative and manipulative, require that individuals first feel comfortable and secure within themselves. But self-awareness is only half the task. Aristotle, I would point out, was certainly one of the most self-aware, self-assured thinkers in history. The scope of his inquiry was encyclopedic; it is claimed that no questions were beyond his scrutiny. Yet the most important question of all—the nature and basis of love—seems to have eluded him completely. "Aristotle," as Bacon so aptly commented, "thought he could not reign secure without putting all his brethren to death."[7] Love, on the other hand, requires that *an individual be able to reign secure at the same time he enables others to reign secure.* I propose that this humanly unifying criterion for love—and *only* this criterion—serve as the common denominator in both the education of our teachers and the education of our youth.

[7] Francis Bacon, *Advancement of Learning*, Book III, Chapter 4, quoted by Will Durant in *The Story of Philosophy*, p. 65.

CHAPTER NINE

THE ANGRY DJINNEE OR SOCRATES?

A famous passage by Terence states that nothing human is foreign. Yet the thinking of the ancient Roman has unreal connotations for many of us living in the midst of a knowledge explosion. In the face of a deluge of data, it is easy for an individual to be overwhelmed by the fear that he cannot be informed—even superficially—on more than an insignificant fraction of available knowledge. However, whereas Terence had the advantage of having to come to grips with a much smaller world of concerns, we who live in the twentieth century have the decided advantage of a fantastic technology—a technology that includes communication devices which have revolutionized ideas about time, space, distance, and speed.

Who among us, for example, watched the historic lunar walk without feeling an intimate part of that great event—without feeling *there*. We did not have to wait years, months, or even hours to get an indirect report of the nature of the moon's surface. Through human ingenuity and the remarkable medium of television, we acquired new knowledge the instant Neil Armstrong took that first "small step" off the ladder of the lunar module. Within seconds, a new door of existence was opened to millions of viewers. Surely the instruments which made this event a part of the experience of us all can give us an intellectual edge over the ancients. In truth there is no reason why the same instruments cannot be used to open new doors of existence on our own globe—a globe which is infinitely more fascinating than the barren, lifeless satellite which has so readily captured our attention.

KNOW-HOW AND MYOPIA

Unfortunately, the intensive specialization of our modern technological world seems to have fragmented the available knowledge and to have created an atmosphere wherein the far-ranging generalist is all too often the object of ridicule by his more specialized and myopic brethren. The specialization which has fostered narrowly circumscribed areas of thought in our laboratories, factories, business houses, military forces, and political offices also has encouraged dreary, restricted thinking in our schools. The typical teacher in the typical classroom is far more concerned with "covering the phylum of biology" than with exploring the quality of life which is lived by biological organisms.[1]

In effect, we are educating legions of persons to live in an extremely incompatible state of affairs. On one hand, the world has become increasingly interdependent; people are starting to talk in terms of "us" rather than "me" and "them." At the same time, the world has become increasingly a place wherein no one is expected to have a view which involves him

---

[1] Cf. the emotional and intellectual poverty of the educational environment depicted in Frederick Wiseman's documentary film *High School* (Cambridge, Mass.: OSTI Films, 1969). See also the results of an extensive, four-year study sponsored by the prestigious Carnegie Corporation: *Crisis in the Classroom* by Charles E. Silberman, pp. 10–11. Silberman's investigating team found American public schools to be "grim, joyless places" with an "intellectually sterile and esthetically barren" atmosphere.

in the whole of anything. With the inevitable diffusion of effort that accompanies a fragmentation of knowledge, we have made it easy for individuals to deny personal responsibility for whatever they help to produce—whether that production involves smog, spaceships, nuclear weapons, computers, grade-point averages, teaching machines, or the caliber of students who are graduated from our educational institutions. In fact, we have thus far succeeded in educating a generation that does not even begin to know what to do with its magnificent technology. Over fifteen years ago, Norbert Wiener stated the issue in biting terms:

Our papers have been making a great deal of American "know-how" ever since we had the misfortune to discover the atomic bomb. There is one quality more important than "know-how" and we cannot excuse the United States of any undue amount of it. This is "know-what" by which we determine not only how to accomplish our purposes, but what our purposes are to be. . . . [The modern American] will accept the superior dexterity of the machine-made decisions without too much inquiry as to the motives and principles behind these. In doing so, he will put himself sooner or later in the position of the father in W. W. Jacobs' *The Monkey's Paw*, who has wished for a hundred pounds, only to find at his door the agent of the company for which his son works, tendering him one hundred pounds as a consolation for his son's death at the factory. Or again, he may do it in the way of the Arab fisherman in the *One Thousand and One Nights*, when he broke the Seal of Solomon on the lid of the bottle which contained the angry djinnee.

Let us remember that there are game-playing machines both of the Monkey's Paw and of the type of the Bottled Djinnee. Any machine constructed for the purpose of making decisions, if it does not possess the power of learning, will be completely literal-minded. Woe to us if we let it decide our conduct, unless we have previously examined the laws of its action, and know fully that its conduct will be carried out on principles acceptable to us! On the other hand, the machine like the djinnee, which can learn and can make decisions on the basis of its learning, will in no way be obliged to make such decisions as we should have made, or will be acceptable to us. For the man who is not aware of this, to throw the problem of his responsibility on the machine, whether it can learn or not, is to cast his responsibility to the winds, and to find it coming back seated on the whirlwind.[2]

Since the reader of this book presumably opened it as part of an inquiry into the know-how of teaching, it would seem appropriate to close on a paraphrase of Wiener's statement: There is one quality more important than know-how, and we cannot excuse American educators of any undue amount of it. That is know-what, by which we determine not only how to accomplish our teaching purposes but what our purposes are to be.

Despite the prevailing lack of concern with know-what and the bleakness of such an atmosphere, I prefer to maintain a positive outlook regarding our individual and collective futures. I believe that we have the option of using our technology to help reactivate the tradition of the classical thinkers, to establish as our most important educational goal the search for truth, goodness, and beauty.

THE UNEXAMINED LIFE . . .

I am aware that this small volume will not create much of a ripple by the newness of its ideas. It is a plea for an ideal that goes back at least as far as Socrates—"*The unexamined life is not worth living!*" Nonetheless I share the optimism of an eloquent spokesman for science who has dared to consider a renewal of this ancient ideal against the challenge of modern technology:

To me, the true significance of the space age, this accelerating age of science and technology in which we now live, is that it is beginning to lead us to wonder, once again, about the nature and purpose of man, about what constitutes the good life and the good society. The space age is bringing philosophy once again to the center of the scene, making it as important as ever it was in the Golden Age of Greece. This is so because the products of science

[2] Norbert Wiener, *The Human Use of Human Beings* (Boston: Houghton Mifflin Co., 1954), pp. 183–85.

and technology offer us the prospect, at last, of satisfying the material needs of all of the people of earth, if we but have the wit and the will to organize and to share our resources.

Moreover, in today's world, concern over the nature and purpose of man need no longer be confined to a small elite with the leisure and the interest. Today it can become the domain of an ever-growing class of people who have the free time, the education and the material resources that are the inevitable products of space-age control of nature by reasonable men.[3]

Certainly if modern man is to live reasonably and significantly, he must learn to live philosophically. By the same token, if the educator is to teach significantly, he must learn to teach philosophically. Who but the educator should have the primary task of triggering off new wonder about the nature and purpose of man, about what constitutes the good life and the good society. And who but the educator ought to prod man into an on-going examination of all his ideas and actions, and the possible implications of his every "small step."

On July 20, 1969, two men stood on the surface of the moon for the first time in history. From their spectacular vantage point in space, these two could look back on the planet earth and view it whole and entire. The age before us holds the promise of re-creating this stirring adventure on a vast scale. But whether or not we as individuals are given an opportunity to move beyond the physically fragmented world of ordinary mortals, we have a desperate need to do so in our thinking. It is my deep hope that the new generation of teachers will feel the intellectual and emotional impact of that grand vision from outer space and will appreciate the wholeness of human life—for themselves as well as for those they teach. I do not deny that such a hope is extravagant. But I agree with Bertrand Russell that modern education seldom achieves a great result because it is so seldom inspired by a great hope.

[3] Walter Orr Roberts, "Science, a Wellspring of Our Discontent," *The American Scholar* (spring, 1967), p. 247.

AN EXISTENTIAL VIEW
OF THE SPECTATOR ROLE

This appendix is included for the purpose of expanding upon the nature of the spectator role referred to in Chapter 3. Generally, the spectator role is associated with realist philosophies because of the rather sharp distinction which they make between the knower and what is known—that is, they regard the person as the beholder of knowledge which exists "out there." In Chapter 3, however, I have suggested that the philosophies of idealism and experimentalism—from an existential point of view—also have a spectator approach. This view warrants further explanation.

THE SPECTATOR ROLE AND IDEALISM

Some commentators would say that idealism emphatically rejects the spectator approach to knowledge. The idealist, for example, believes that the world is an expression of a moving spirit—and that all things in the world, including man, are expressions of the same spiritual reality. Thus, rather than seeing man as a spectator of external events in an impersonal world, he views man as a creature with a given destiny—an intimate part of a friendly and personal world, the organic whole of which is perceived as growing toward a common transempirical ideal. This ideal usually is portrayed as a Supreme Being or as the Absolute Mind one finds in Hegel's dialectic conception of the world.[1]

To the existentialist, the idealist world-view is akin to a negation of individuality and personal freedom. The implication is that the self has an immanent nature which *must* harmonize with a grand design of the universe. Hence the only choice presented to the individual is in the limited sense of choosing not to harmonize. The grand design, to the existentialist, is an artificial, externalized construct. And, in relationship to this construct, he feels that a person assumes an onlooker or spectator role rather than *making himself*.

THE SPECTATOR ROLE AND EXPERIMENTALISM

Some would also disagree with me in ascribing the spectator relationship to experimentalism, since that philosophy expresses much regard for subjective perceptions of reality and internalized learning. But in experimentalism there is a powerful tradition of social evolution and a belief that living the good life involves a natural, progressive adaptation by the individual to the common aims, beliefs, and aspirations of the total society. This social development toward similar emotional and intellectual dispositions (that is, toward a consensus of thinking in vital matters) is seen as necessary to ensure that individuals will work together as an enlightened social group. To achieve social control through common understanding is held to be the prime function of education; it boils down to a guidance and redirection of the natural impulses of the young toward the life customs of the larger society. Since espousal of "social norms" (which undergo continuous reappraisal within this evolutionary world-view) is sought through

[1] Cf. S. Samuel Shermis, *Philosophic Foundations of Education*, p. 251.

mutual understanding and identity of interests on the part of all the members of a society rather than through intellectual or emotional compulsion, the process is held to be neither external nor coercive.[2]

From an existentialist's point of view, the experimentalist's idea of internally and naturally redirecting one's life and thought toward the normative thinking of an evolving social order represents a fundamental contradiction. For him, the goal of an overall social like-mindedness ignores the *intrinsic uniqueness* of all persons, who are thrown into varying existential world situations where there is no guarantee whatsoever of a natural evolution toward "social progress." A "like-minded" social aim, the existentialist feels, suggests that an individual ought to assume a posture of detachment from himself in order to conform to compelling social norms—norms which may violate his own private being and integrity.

THE SPECTATOR ROLE AND SOCIAL DEVELOPMENTALISM

In further exploring the above ideas, I refer my reader to Robert Nisbet's penetrating analysis of the impact of the social development theory on Western thinking and values.[3] Nisbet painstakingly demonstrates that developmentalism is one of the oldest Western ideas. It has been incorporated, for example, into the social theories of the pre-Socratic Greeks, Platonists, Aristotelians, Augustinians, Enlightenment thinkers, Darwinists, Marxists, as well as the functionalists, who dominate the social sciences in our own era of history (see Nisbet, pages 228–232). One social theory after another, he argues, has been a variation of the same fundamental assumption: Societies are organic wholes that change gradually, cumulatively, and irreversibly "through a kind of unfolding of internal potentiality, the whole moving toward some end that is presumably contained in the process from the start" (page

[2] See, e.g., John Dewey, *Democracy and Education*, pp. 1–40; and John Dewey, *Reconstruction in Philosophy*, pp. 205–11.

[3] Robert A. Nisbet, *Social Change and History: Aspects of the Western Theory of Development*.

3). This, of course, is the very tradition which undergirds both idealist and experimentalist philosophies. Despite the fact that the latter philosophy disclaims any transempirical or mystical force in providing motive power for social progress, its reliance on experimental (empirical) science as a cumulative directing source for "improving" societies and cultures serves essentially the same purpose.

Now the crux of the developmental theory, as Nisbet points out, is that no one ever has empirically witnessed (as one might observe such things in the world of plants and animals) a development of societies and cultures. To Nisbet, the whole theory of social development is a metaphor. As observed by the existentialist, it is a popular article of faith, a doctrine to which he refuses to subscribe because it invariably shifts freedom and responsibility away from him toward collectivized thinking. The existentialist pictures himself in a world that is not evolving in any particular direction. Societies, as he sees them, follow neither inherently dynamic nor static patterns. Whatever societal design might be evidenced, it is of man's own making.

In any event, the existentialist believes that he possesses no natural impulses which compel him to tune in to collectivized human movements—whether these movements are restricted to the empirical world or have transempirical implications. He is, in short, *an arbitrary organism*, who, despite the existence of causal circumstances in his life, *always* is confronted with the possibility of alternative behavior and indeterminate choice. To ask the existentialist to believe otherwise is to ask him to accept a passive, subordinate, and dispassionate role in life instead of claiming control over his destiny to the fullest possible extent.

NOT SIMPLY A MATTER OF DOING ONE'S OWN THING

The comments in this appendix are included for the benefit of the reader who comes away from the nine chapters of this volume under the impression that I sanction a *laissez faire* approach to classroom teaching. Let the record be clear on this: I do not regard teaching in terms of an *isolated* doing one's own thing, nor do I see learning simply as a spontaneous happening. The two broad recommendations which follow are offered to further clarify my ideas regarding the academic freedom of an individual teacher within the cooperative enterprise of the American public school system.

THE USE OF CURRICULUM GUIDES AND OTHER PLANNING INSTRUMENTS

One distinguished educator recently quipped that the only persons who learn anything from curriculum guides are the people who put them together in the first place.[1] His comment

[1] From an address by Richard L. Foster, "Educational Supervision: Dead or Alive," given before the annual conference of the Association for Supervision and Curriculum Development, Chicago, March, 1969.

surely is warranted. Next to doctoral dissertations, school curriculum guides probably gather a heavier layer of dust than any other type of reading matter. This is a waste of a resource valuable to the classroom teacher. I suggest that the *curriculum guide* is the first of a series of planning instruments which can be used to provide the teacher with an extremely helpful overview of the entire school program. Moreover, the curriculum guide, along with the other planning instruments derived therefrom, can provide the teacher with a concrete yet flexible basis from which to organize his own course.

Since curriculum guides frequently serve as the butt of teachers' jokes about "administrative meddling" and are often regarded as unwelcome, ironclad dictums of what each teacher is "expected to cover," let me clarify my remarks about these instruments. In brief, I regard a curriculum guide as precisely that—*a guide, not a directive.* If a teacher sees the curriculum guide as a restrictive device, the chances are high that he regards the guide in the same unfortunate way that many teachers regard a textbook—as the curriculum master instead of a tool which they can utilize (along with many other tools) in a highly personal, creative manner.

Let us assume, for example, that a teacher has been assigned to teach a senior-level course in economics. Let us further assume that this teacher wants to build his course on the basis of his students' previous educational experiences— that is, he wants to help his students grasp the significance of economics in relationship to some of the learning experiences they already have had. Upon inquiry the teacher will likely discover that his school district has developed a curriculum guide or a series of guides in his particular area of study. These guides usually are compiled by groups of teachers within the school system, often under the direction of a curriculum administrator. Typically, school districts develop an individual curriculum guide for each area of study—that is, one for science, English, social studies, physical education, etc. These areas, in turn, are grouped by academic level. One curriculum guide might be designated for use in grades 7, 8, and 9 and another in grades 10, 11, and 12. Some districts publish combined junior and senior high school curriculum guides. Occasionally, the entire K-12 curriculum for a particular subject will be given within a single publication; however, at least a thumbnail sketch of the K-12 program generally will appear in the introductory pages of each guide.

Whatever the physical appearance, curriculum guides represent an attempt to *loosely structure* a subject to discourage blind repetition of earlier course offerings and to facilitate a fairly sequential presentation of a particular subject during the students' K-12 years. Therefore, in reviewing such a guide, our economics teacher not only is put in touch with some broad guidelines in terms of the recommended substance of his own course but is likely to discover numerous ideas about economics that have been treated in, say, the seventh- and tenth-grade programs and which conceivably could be reintroduced and related to more sophisticated economic ideas in his twelfth-grade course.

I am aware that experienced teachers frequently complain that students "never remember much" from previous classes, and therefore the use of curriculum guides may seem unrealistic to them. But I am equally aware that few teachers presently make a continuing effort to interrelate student learnings beyond the limits of their own course. And since students, like most people, do not do a particularly good job of remembering whatever appears to have no demonstrable ongoing importance to them, it is not at all surprising—in view of the prevailing learning climate—that they fail to perceive a connection between what happened in one of their seventh-grade classes and the topic under consideration in a twelfth-grade class. In short, I am suggesting that the negative reactions of teachers to curriculum guides stem more from teaching-myopia than from learning capacities of students.

As is true of all the planning instruments I will mention, curriculum guides have no set pattern. Some school districts develop rather elaborate guides of encyclopedia proportions; others publish modest pamphlets. Some guides are written in flowing, descriptive prose; others contain terse phrases in outline form. But whatever the detail, curriculum guides usually list general learning objectives and recommend general topics of study to be treated in particular courses, segmenting these topics into smaller units. The nebulous nature of the learning objectives which typically appear in the pages of curriculum guides may be distressing to the reader if he recalls the discussion of "glittering generalities" in Chapter 3. However, I would remind him of the positive aspect of such statements—namely, the freedom afforded the individual teacher in bringing substantive meaning to these objectives from his *own* philosophic orientation. If, for example, the teacher operates from a positivist-realist tradition, nothing need prevent him from tightening up the phrasing of the objectives he uses for guidelines, perhaps even to writing them all out in the precise behavioral fashion.

Depending on the district that issues it, the curriculum guide may be detailed enough to fulfill the function of the second planning instrument—the *course of study*. Otherwise, this is likely to appear as an accompanying publication. The course of study, as the name implies, focuses on a single-semester or two-semester course—for example, twelfth-grade economics. Like the larger curriculum guide, the course of study may be the result of teacher collaboration within the school system or the compilation of curriculum experts employed by the school district. In smaller systems, the course of study may be the responsibility of a single teacher, particularly if he is the only one assigned to teach such a course.

Since our economics teacher must plan his course to run a designated number of teaching days, he will need to block out some tentative ideas about what content will be taken up and approximately how much time the class will spend on the various studies. The course of study, with its recommended learning objectives and outline of content, as well as its corresponding suggestions for resources and activities, can give the teacher a starting place from which to map out his course. Exercising his professional judgment, the economics teacher might determine what seems to him a much better sequence for handling the recommended content of the course. Also, he might decide to build his course around only three, let us say, of the ten major topics suggested in the course of study, perhaps planning to touch upon the remaining topics only as he can relate them to the three in-depth studies. As he views his own course *within the context of the full curriculum*, he undoubtedly will want to alter the official course of study in terms of his own ideas about economics and his own perceptions of twelfth-grade students.

Once the teacher has roughed out his own course of study and has decided upon a tentative time schedule, his next task is to develop the smaller segments of the course—the units of study. In this process, our economics teacher can make use of another planning instrument, the *resource unit*. Typically it is included in the makeup of a course of study. However, it is not uncommon for special resource units to be prepared for use in conjunction with designated courses of study. Again, such resource units might be official publications of a school system or the result of the informal efforts of several teachers.

Written in considerable detail, the resource unit ordinarily contains a listing of proposed learning objectives (again typically phrased as "glittering generalities") and an outline of content abstracted from the course of study. In addition, the resource unit includes rather extensive, specific suggestions of ways in which the unit content can be introduced to a class, how it can be developed, and how the unit activities might be culminated. Usually incorporated into a resource unit are listings and sources of teaching aids—both recommended reading materials and audio-visual materials related to the unit of study.

The curriculum guide, course of study, and resource units developed within his own school system are not the only planning instruments available to our economics teacher. In the process of developing his own curriculum perspective and exposing himself to a broad range of ideas on content and methodology, he will find it advantageous to procure copies of planning instruments from *other* school systems across the country. Generally these can be obtained at nominal expense from the administrative offices of the school systems. State departments of education frequently develop planning instruments for the benefit of classroom teachers; therefore, curriculum personnel in the nation's fifty state departments can serve as valuable resource people to the teacher.

In addition, professional organizations such as the Association for Supervision and Curriculum Development, National Education Association, National Council of Teachers of Mathematics, National Council for the Social Studies, National Council of Teachers of English, National Art Education Association, National Science Teachers Association, National Business Education Association, American Association for Health, Physical Education, and Recreation, etc., publish floods of curriculum materials which provide a wealth of ideas. If the teacher lives in the vicinity of a college or university which houses a school of education, he is likely to find that the library there includes a "curriculum materials library"—essentially a collection of curriculum guides, courses of study, and sample resource units obtained from professional organizations, state departments of education, and school districts throughout the country. Needless to say, such a library service is a useful resource for the classroom teacher.

Since any individual's private well of ideas will run dry with daily pumping, the innovative and exciting teacher will find it easier to remain so if he leaves his thinking open to a variety of professional sources, as well as to the ideas of his own students. In harmony with the theory of curriculum content selection and development presented in Chapter 4,[2] I would reemphasize my own belief that the teacher's personal philosophy should play the determining role. Nonetheless, I consider the use of a wide assortment of planning instruments indispensable in giving the teacher a broad perspective within which his own belief system can function intelligently in a pluralistic teaching-learning environment.

In the event that the reader questions whether the use of curriculum guides is compatible with the general theme of teacher freedom argued throughout this book, let me refer him back to the "clearinghouse" discussion in Chapter 4.[3]

[2] See pp. 80–87.
[3] See pp. 79–80.

The clearinghouse operation of all our social institutions implies that information is shared among the members in an atmosphere of authentic interaction, that broad policy-making is arrived at on the basis of group efforts to find points of accommodation, and that most criteria for decision-making ultimately reside with individuals in specific situations. I regard curriculum guides and other curriculum-planning instruments as bases for promoting this kind of interaction within our schools—no more and no less.

THE CASE FOR WRITTEN PLANS

Probably few aspects of pre-service teacher education are approached with the cynicism accorded to written planning. To be blunt, this cynicism on the part of the education student is justified. More frequently than not he observes contradictory practices in his own college classes; and as he steps into his student-teaching assignment with serious ideas about advance preparation, he often is advised that teaching is better played by ear or that few teachers have the time to organize elaborate plans that only have to be changed daily anyway. Consequently, many student teachers find themselves caught in a credibility gap between the university supervisor, who is likely to insist on unit and lesson planning, and the critic teacher in the public school, who regards this kind of planning as busywork. Therefore, unless the student teacher is convinced in the early stages of his career of the necessity for careful advance planning, the chances are high that he will follow in the footsteps of the vast majority of practicing teachers—that is, he will regard long-range designing of classroom activities as superfluous. Or he is likely to rationalize that detailed planning may be necessary for the novice teacher but is a waste of time for the experienced one.

It is true that few teachers delight in the difficult, unending work of developing unit and lesson plans. However, it would be foolish to negate the critical importance of these tools simply because they require considerable effort on the teacher's part. It is my opinion that classroom teachers, *regardless of the number of years they have spent in the classroom,* need to develop both long-range written plans and daily written plans.

The recommendation that teachers maintain written records as part of their professional responsibilities is very much in harmony with procedures that are accepted as a matter of course within other professions. Lawyers, for example, spend considerably more time in researching and writing legal briefs than in arguing their cases before courts of law. To suggest that even a highly experienced lawyer enter a courtroom without careful advance preparation or with his ideas merely in his head would be nonsensical. From countless observations, I am convinced that a teacher who attempts to function with a hastily conceived and sloppily executed lesson plan is as effective in a classroom as a lawyer in a courtroom with a sloppy brief.

The attitude of the teacher toward unit and lesson plans will be strongly affected by the way in which he sees their function—that is, whether he regards them as rigid formats which foster canned presentations or as *flexible guides* which establish tentative content and procedures but which can be readily revamped as the class develops. Suppose, for example, a junior high school science teacher arrives in class to find his students excitedly examining a turtle, and his lesson plan for the day is about crabs. When the bell rings, only the teacher's insensitivity and lack of imagination will cause him to order his students to put away the turtle and concentrate on the planned lesson. The creative teacher, I submit, will flex his thinking in order to *start* with the turtle, adjusting his lesson plan on the spot. This, however, is not the same as advocating that a teacher arrive before his students each day with an expectant, "What are you interested in?" or "What would you like to do today?" Below I have outlined the key arguments, as I see them, for the practice of writing out daily lesson plans. I encourage the reader to assess the merits of these ideas carefully:

First, the teacher needs to be able to justify to himself whatever he does in class and whatever he would like to have his students do. Furthermore, he needs to be able to communicate these underlying whys to his students in a way that makes good sense *to them*. Since the teacher, like most human beings, tends to live, work, and communicate with other people from an egocentric orientation, the justification for classroom activities generally will reflect whys which satisfy his own orientation rather than that of the student. I am suggesting that a major advantage of written plans is that they require much greater in-depth pre-thought on the part of the teacher in terms of where the class is going and why—pre-thought that can help him break through his own orientation and see the learning situation through the eyes of his students.

Where the class is going, of course, is intimately tied to the underlying why. For example, the direction of study might be the result of the teacher's conviction that students need to possess a prescribed, fixed body of historical knowledge—perhaps "an understanding of the five major causes of the Second World War." Or the direction of study might be shaped by the teacher's belief that historical inquiry is an open, interpretive phenomenon and that it is helpful for students, in the process of developing a perspective on their own lives, to have a feel for the speculative nature of the human story. The latter teacher, for example, might want students to develop "an understanding of the multiple and extremely complex causes of the Second World War and the possible implications for Americans living in the contemporary era." But whether the proposed direction is fixed and closed or speculative and open, the significance of the study invariably will be lost to students unless the teacher deliberately orients the study in the light of his own genuine insights into the experiential background of his students—their existing knowledge, values, interests, and concerns. This does not imply that he must encourage students to remain where they are in their thinking, but it does mean that he will need to initiate a study *where his students presently are*. Beyond that, where the class might go is limited only by the teacher's own lack of purpose, creativity, and foresight.

In this crucial matter of content orientation, I recall an experience I had as a first-year high school teacher of social studies. After my first few weeks in the classroom, I decided to scrap the kind of detailed lesson plans I had used throughout my student teaching assignment. The lesson plan I adopted now that my university supervisor was no longer peering over my shoulder consisted of a few content ideas. Since I thought I knew the material to be examined in class, it seemed to me that a simple listing of content in the sequence of presentation and discussion was sufficient to move my classes into high gear of meaningful learning.

One of the early topics I posed for class consideration was the ancient Middle Eastern civilizations. Because of my own deep interest and excitement over human history of all eras, I had selected the content and launched into the unit of study with great enthusiasm. It was quite a blow one day when an unhappy voice from the back of the room broke the flow of discussion with, "Why the heck do we have to study about the Babylonians?" For someone who had spent four years in concentrated study of the Babylonians and other groups, the why seemed crystal clear. So I proceeded to explain why to the entire class and rapidly found myself floundering around for a rationale that had some basis of appeal beyond my own particular interests.

It did not take long for me to realize that despite my knowledge of the topic, I had not worked through the significance of such a study from the students' point of view. Nor had I worked through ways in which I might possibly hook and sustain my students' interest in ideas and events that were bound to appear remote and irrelevant from the context of their world. Consequently, the level of meaningful communication in that class was very low, and it became increasingly clear that my presentation of the Babylonians had elicited little more than a "So what!" response.

This experience helped to illuminate a number one reality of classroom teaching: Whereas I could continue to seek inspiration and to select curriculum content from my own frame of reference, in order to have meaningful communication with my students it was *also* necessary that I project myself into their frames of reference. I realized further that this projection and the resultant translation of content into activities relevant for students were not automatic by-products of scholarly research and teaching erudition. Nor were they likely to occur without considerable foresight and experimentation on my part. I subsequently discovered that carefully written plans could be valuable instruments in helping me to consider *my students* as I organized learning activities. By writing down the how of my teaching (for example, visual aids, pivotal questions, demonstrations, group work) in addition to the what, or content, I could see at a glance whether or not my methods were falling into a dull, repetitious routine or whether they were varied and interesting. Also, I had a visual check as to whether I was making a concerted effort to relate the content to the experiential backgrounds of the students. I do not mean that I found written plans to be automatic guarantees of "good" lessons, but they did serve as constant reminders of the learning problems faced by students when they are exposed to a steady diet of verbal abstractions. In a word, the habit of advance lesson planning—that is, a careful, deliberate projection of both *content and method*—helped me to keep in mind a common mistake that teachers make:

It is to present students with our own carefully thought out conclusions when they themselves lack the raw experience from which these conclusions are fashioned. . . . Much of the intellectual apathy we complain about is due to our fault of presenting conclusions in lieu of first-hand experience. To us, our well-chiseled conclusion, summing up a long intellectual struggle with a problem of knowledge or of value, seems like a beautiful sonnet. To the student, it may be gibberish.[4]

A *second* major consideration which supports the practice of using written plans is that the teacher needs to cope with the factor of on-going change in his field of study and in the background, interests, and abilities of individual students. There is simply no single, permanent way of organizing and handling curriculum content. Thus written planning has the

[4] Gordon W. Allport, "Values and Our Youth," *Teachers College Record* (December, 1961), p. 218.

advantage of encouraging in-depth consideration of how to meet each new teaching situation. Expressed another way, freshly written plans facilitate a reconstruction of the teacher's thinking and his resolution of new ideas, knowledge, and interpretations. The novice teacher who enters the classroom for the first time will do so with a reservoir of freshly minted ideas. But he needs to be aware that his reservoir will dry up quickly if he does not leave himself open to new learnings— learnings that should make his original teaching plans obsolete.

Most of us are familiar with teachers who use written plans that have yellowed with age. At the same time, most of us could single out teachers who require no written plans at all because their teaching—both content and methodology—consists of routine, force-of-habit presentations. I would suggest that the supreme test of the on-going growth so necessary for effective teaching is the degree of comfort one finds in reviewing old unit and lesson plans. Although old plans can be good references in building and revising a course of study, a teacher should be jarred if his plans fit him like a glove with the second use.

A *third* justification for written plans is that students themselves have an appreciation of teachers who come to class with apparent advance preparation. It is my custom to recommend to student teachers that they subject themselves to a detailed critique by their students at the end of their student teaching experience. With remarkable consistency, one area that students single out for special comment is whether the teacher gave evidence of being well prepared each day. Students tend to object strenuously if written plans are used as intellectual strait jackets and if the teacher focuses attention upon his plans to the neglect of his students. But on the other hand, students find great merit in written plans which are used by a teacher to map out new territories for the class to explore.

Fourth and finally, written plans help to develop some degree of continuity within the total curriculum. Since life outside the school is integrated and not comprised of separate topics of inquiry, there is a need to help students integrate their learning experiences *within* the school. For example, what a student has been exposed to in a junior English course should have a recognized relationship to what he does in the senior course. And what the student does in all his English classes ought to have a relationship to what goes on within his other courses. If the interrelationships among the student's various learning experiences are not consciously sought by all those persons involved in the educational enterprise, the chances are slim that the student ever will feel the necessity of synthesizing his knowledge. Yet it is only when a student is able to pull his knowledge together into a meaningful whole that his formal education will serve him as the basis for an intelligent, mature, and integrated life.

Unfortunately, however, teachers don't always communicate well on curriculum matters with other faculty members, let alone with students, administrators, school board members, and parents. Consequently, the understanding of the teaching staff itself regarding what each teacher is doing and how his efforts fit into the total picture of education is often nebulous. In my opinion, the failure to commit individual teaching plans to writing is one major reason for this problem of poor communication. Staff meetings held to improve the curriculum and to integrate student learnings usually generate pointless and frustrating discussion when teachers are without concrete, detailed curriculum materials to exchange, examine, and interrelate. It is foolish for teachers to attempt to function in isolation since their students are educated within the larger system of the school. If teachers are interested in avoiding a fragmentation of their students' learning experiences within the total curriculum, *it is imperative that they communicate with one another about the specifics of their classroom activities.*

This is *not* to suggest staff agreement in the specifics of content selection, organization, and treatment. As pointed out repeatedly in this book, there is a wide latitude for independent teacher judgment in these matters. However, on-going communication is essential if each educator within the school system is to have an *awareness* of all the learning experiences to which his students are exposed. Inter-staff communication is also necessary in view of the fact that the education of our youth is an extraordinarily complex task. Many curriculum decisions must be hammered out on the basis of multiple talents, opinions, and energies.

An overriding theme of this book is the desirability of a loosely structured curriculum wherein the uniqueness of individual teachers has room for experimentation and innovation in the classroom. However, the paradox posed by the concept of cultural pluralism is that individuality and uniqueness need to be fostered at the same time as cooperation, which is needed to enable individuals to work together in group situations. The school system, of course, is a group situation, one which involves teachers, administrators, students, parents, school board members, and the community at large. Consequently, many of the decisions involved in the operation of this system should result from deliberations among all members of that system. A determination that the sophomore year of mathematics will be concerned with geometry and the junior year with algebra, for example, is not a decision which ought to be the prerogative of any one person. Policies of class size, course scheduling, and graduation requirements are other examples of matters which properly should lie beyond the decision-making responsibilities of a single individual. Group determination of such problems obviously is necessary if a school is to avoid the two extremes of curriculum chaos and curriculum dictatorship.

The dual function of a teacher as an individual committed to a total personal philosophy of education and as a member of a large system composed of many diverse ways of thinking may seem to pose an irreconcilable dilemma. Many a courageous teacher has gone out on an innovative limb only to find it sawed off. Because few teachers want to risk martyrdom in terms of loss of professional status and even loss of their positions, most of them passively acquiesce in the curriculum decisions of the total group—a group which frequently serves as an organ of expression only for the dominant members.

I believe that the delicate balance between the teacher's

personal prerogatives and his group responsibilities in curriculum matters can be reconciled if the teacher consciously and consistently avoids creating a narcissistic atmosphere in his working relationships. This does not imply that the teacher (or anyone else within the system for that matter) should refrain from promoting group interest in and support of his ideas. But it does suggest that such promotion should not be of the allness-or-else variety which sets out to destroy the thinking of other individuals. Scores of educators make the mistake of trying to implement new curriculum ideas *at the expense of other people*. When such experiments backfire, as they generally do, the tendency is for the would-be innovator either to retreat in frustration or to try to force others to accept his point of view. Each teacher must recognize that many of the innovations he wants to try out will have repercussions beyond his own immediate sphere of operation. Consequently, he needs to be very sensitive to the beliefs, interests, and convictions of other individuals within the total system. If he wishes to win group approval for his ideas, he will be ill advised to approach those other individuals (whether fellow teachers, students, administrators, parents, school-board members, or the community at large) in an abrasive, demeaning manner or in any way that conveys a belittling, superior-inferior attitude toward their biases and behavior.

On the other hand, once a particular course of action is decided upon by the group, I submit that the individual teacher should be guaranteed the freedom to continue to question the efficacy of such action. In other words, *the right of continuing dissent*—and the corresponding right to encourage a reexamination of a particular curriculum policy enacted by the rest of the group—should be respected as a necessary way of life among professional educators no less than among all other individuals within a democratic society. If such dissent is encouraged and not stifled, no teacher need feel that he is a victim of the tyranny of the majority or that he has to compromise his deeply held convictions—even though he may find it necessary to abide by the group decision on some issues at a particular time.[5] In essence, I am reemphasizing the idea expressed in Chapter 4, namely, that any teacher has the ability and the ultimate right to choose his own attitude, if not always his physical actions, in any given situation.

But, again, the kind of professional exchange of ideas that I am calling for here will be greatly facilitated if the classroom teacher gets into the habit of maintaining written plans and then makes a policy of sharing his teaching experiences with his colleagues. This posture sharply deviates from typical teaching behavior, which advocates that the best way for the teacher to "beat the system" is to retreat to his classroom, close the door, and operate within those four walls as if he were dealing with one master, one fate, and one soul.

[5] Cf. Richard L. Tobin's discussion of the need in a democratic society "to require opportunity for expression as well as protection for expression once secured." See "The Omnipotence of the Majority," p. 18. See also Alexis de Tocqueville's classic, sobering statement warning against a "tyranny of the majority": *Democracy in America*, trans. George Lawrence, eds. J. P. Mayer and Max Lerner, pp. 227–40.

BIBLIOGRAPHY

CHAPTER 1

Bow, James. "School Shake-up Could Help: Finch." *Denver Post,* January 7, 1969, p. 10.

Cass, James. "Profit and Loss in Education." *Saturday Review,* August 15, 1970, pp. 39–40.

"Collision Course in the High Schools." *Life,* May 16, 1969, pp. 22–39.

Committee on Assessing the Progress of Education. *How Much Are Students Learning? Plans for a National Assessment of Education.* Ann Arbor, Mich.: The Committee, 1968.

Divoky, Diane. "Revolt in the High Schools: The Way It's Going to Be." *Saturday Review,* February 15, 1969, p. 83.

"Free Enterprise for Schools," *Time,* August 24, 1970, pp. 58–59.

Gershoy, Leo. *The French Revolution and Napoleon.* New York: Appleton-Century-Crofts, 1964.

Joint Committee on Testing: American Association of School Administrators, Council of Chief State School Officers, National Association of Secondary School Principals. *Testing, Testing, Testing.* Washington, D.C.: National Education Association, 1962.

Maxwell, John, and Anthony Tovatt, eds. *On Writing Behavioral Objectives for English.* Champaign, Ill.: National Council of Teachers of English, 1970.

Merton, Robert K. *Social Theory and Social Structure.* New York: Free Press, 1968.

Nelson, Jack, and Gene Roberts, Jr. *The Censors and the Schools.* Boston: Little, Brown and Co., 1963.

"Nixon Proposes School Reform," *Denver Post,* March 3, 1970, p. 1.

Reich, Charles A. *The Greening of America.* New York: Random House, 1970.

Ridgeway, James. "Computer-Tutor," *New Republic,* June 4, 1966, p. 19.

Roszak, Theodore. *The Making of a Counter Culture.* Garden City, N.Y.: Doubleday & Co., 1969.

CHAPTER 2

ASCD Yearbook Committee. *Perceiving, Behaving, Becoming.* Washington, D.C.: Association for Supervision and Curriculum Development, 1962.

Carnegie, Andrew. *The Gospel of Wealth.* New York: Century Co., 1900.

Chilcott, John H., Norman C. Greenberg, and Herbert B. Wilson, eds. *Readings in the Socio-Cultural Foundations of Education.* Belmont, Calif.: Wadsworth Publishing Co., 1968.

Fincher, Jack. "The Hog-Tied Brig Brats of Camp Pendleton." *Life,* October 10, 1969, pp. 32–37.

Frankl, Viktor E. *Man's Search for Meaning.* New York: Washington Square Press, 1963.

Friedenberg, Edgar Z. *The Vanishing Adolescent.* New York: Dell Publishing Co., 1959.

Greene, Maxine, ed. *Existential Encounters for Teachers.* New York: Random House, 1967.

Harris, Sidney J. *Majority of One.* Boston: Houghton Mifflin Co., 1957.

Heisenberg, Werner. *The Physicist's Conception of Nature.* Translated by Arnold J. Pomerans. New York: Harcourt Brace Jovanovich, 1955.

Henry, Nelson B., ed. *Modern Philosophies and Education.* Fifty-fourth Yearbook of the National Society for the Study of Education. Chicago: University of Chicago Press, 1955.

Hoffmann, Banesh. *The Strange Story of the Quantum,* 2nd ed. New York: Dover Publications, 1959.

Kennedy, John F. *A Nation of Immigrants.* New York: Popular Library, 1964.

Krutch, Joseph Wood. *The Measure of Man.* Indianapolis: Bobbs-Merrill Co., 1953.

Liegerot, Giles F. "Is Academic Competition for You?" *National Association of Secondary-School Principals Bulletin,* November, 1961, pp. 148–52.

Lifton, Robert J. "Beyond Atrocity." *Saturday Review,* March 27, 1971, pp. 23–25, 54.

Lorenz, Konrad. *On Aggression*. New York: Harcourt Brace Jovanovich, 1966.

Marcel, Gabriel. *Man against Mass Society*. Chicago: Henry Regnery Co., 1962.

"The Massacre at Mylai." *Life*, December 5, 1969, pp. 36–45.

May, Rollo. *Love and Will*. New York: W. W. Norton & Co., 1969.

McCullock, Frank. "The Fall of a 'Lost Soldier.'" *Life*, November 28, 1969, pp. 17–19.

Miller, Perry, ed. *American Thought: Civil War to World War I*. New York: Holt, Rinehart and Winston, 1964.

Montagu, M. F. Ashley. *The Direction of Human Development*. New York: Harper & Row, 1955.

Morris, Desmond. *The Human Zoo*. New York: McGraw-Hill Book Co., 1969.

———. *The Naked Ape*. New York: McGraw-Hill Book Co., 1967.

Morris, Van Cleve, ed. *Modern Movements in Educational Philosophy*. Boston: Houghton Mifflin Co., 1969.

Moustakas, Clark. *Creativity and Conformity*. Princeton, N.J.: D. Van Nostrand Co., 1967.

Nisbet, Robert A. *Social Change and History: Aspects of the Western Theory of Development*. London: Oxford University Press, 1969.

Petersen, Aage. *Quantum Physics and the Philosophical Tradition*. Cambridge: Massachusetts Institute of Technology, 1968.

Phenix, Philip H., ed. *Philosophies of Education*. New York: John Wiley & Sons, 1961.

Planck, Max. *A Survey of Physics*. New York: E. P. Dutton and Co., 1925.

Riesman, David, Nathan Glazer, and Reuel Denney. *The Lonely Crowd*. New London, Conn.: Yale University Press, 1950.

Rogers, Carl R. *On Becoming a Person*. Boston: Houghton Mifflin Co., 1961.

Skinner, B. F. *The Technology of Teaching*. New York: Appleton-Century-Crofts, 1968.

———. *Walden Two*. New York: Macmillan Co., 1948; paperback Macmillan, 1962.

Snygg, Donald, and Arthur Combs. *Individual Behavior*. New York: Harper & Brothers, 1949.

Whyte, William H., Jr., *The Organization Man*. New York: Simon and Schuster, 1956.

CHAPTER 3

Bambrough, Renford. *The Philosophy of Aristotle*. New York: Mentor Books, 1963.

Barnett, Lincoln. *The Universe and Dr. Einstein*, 2nd rev. ed. New York: Mentor Books, 1957.

Barzun, Jacques. *Teacher in America*. Boston: Little, Brown and Co., 1945.

Bigge, Morris L., and Maurice P. Hunt. *Psychological Foundations of Education*. New York: Harper & Row, 1962.

Bridgman, P. W. "Philosophical Implications of Physics." *The American Academy of Arts and Science Bulletin*, February, 1950.

Broudy, Harry S., and John R. Palmer. *Exemplars of Teaching Method*. Chicago: Rand McNally & Co., 1965.

Bruner, Jerome. *The Process of Education*. Cambridge: Harvard University Press, 1960; paperback Vintage Books, 1960.

Butler, J. Donald. *Four Philosophies and Their Practice in Education and Religion*, 3rd ed. New York: Harper & Row, 1968.

Clinchy, Blythe. "The Role of Intuition in Learning." *NEA Journal*, February, 1968, p. 33.

Commission on the Reorganization of Secondary Education. *Cardinal Principles of Secondary Education*. United States Office of Education Bulletin No. 35. Washington, D.C.: Government Printing Office, 1918.

Conant, James B. *Modern Science and Modern Man*. New York: Columbia University Press, 1952.

Dewey, John. *How We Think*. Boston: D.C. Heath and Co., 1933.

Educational Policies Commission. *The Central Purpose of American Education*. Washington: National Education Association, 1961.

————. *Education for All American Youth*. Washington: National Education Association, 1944.

————. *Education for All American Youth: A Further Look*. Washington: National Education Association, 1954.

————. *The Purposes of Education in American Democracy*. Washington: National Education Association, 1938.

Gamow, George. *Matter, Earth, and Sky*. Englewood Cliffs, N.J.: Prentice-Hall, 1958.

Geiger, George R. *Philosophy and the Social Order*. Boston: Houghton Mifflin Co., 1947.

Greene, Maxine, ed. *Existential Encounters for Teachers*. New York: Random House, 1967.

Grieder, Calvin, and Stephen Romine. *American Education*, 3d ed. New York: Ronald Press Co., 1965.

Heisenberg, Werner. *The Physicist's Conception of Nature*. Translated by Arnold J. Pomerans. New York: Harcourt Brace Jovanovich, 1955.

Henry, Nelson B., ed. *Modern Philosophies and Education*. Fifty-fourth Yearbook of the National Society for the Study of Education. Chicago: University of Chicago Press, 1955.

Hutchins, Robert Maynard. *The Higher Learning in America*. New Haven: Yale University Press, 1936.

Kneller, George F. *Introduction to the Philosophy of Education*. New York: John Wiley & Sons, 1964.

Koch, Adrienne, and William Peden. *The Life and Selected Writings of Thomas Jefferson*. New York: Modern Library, 1944.

Leonard, George B. *Education and Ecstasy*. New York: Delacorte Press, 1968.

Massialas, Byron G., and Andreas M. Kazamias, eds. *Crucial Issues in the Teaching of Social Studies*. Englewood Cliffs, N.J.: Prentice-Hall, 1964.

Morris, Van Cleve, ed. *Modern Movements in Educational Philosophy*. Boston: Houghton Mifflin Co., 1969.

Phenix, Philip H., ed. *Philosophies of Education*. New York: John Wiley & Sons, 1961.

Van Doren, Mark. *Liberal Education.* New York: Henry Holt and Co., 1943; paperback Beacon Press, 1959.

Wharton, John F. "Does Anyone Know Reality?" *Saturday Review,* December 3, 1966, pp. 21–23.

CHAPTER 4

Buber, Martin. *I and Thou.* Translated by Ronald G. Smith. New York: Charles Scribner's Sons, 1937.

Butler, J. Donald. *Four Philosophies and Their Practice in Education and Religion,* 3d ed. New York: Harper & Row, 1968.

Dewey, John. *Art as Experience.* New York: Minton, Balch & Co., 1934.

Frankl, Viktor E. *Man's Search for Meaning.* New York: Washington Square Press, 1963.

Galbraith, John Kenneth. *The New Industrial State.* Boston: Houghton Mifflin Co., 1967.

Goodman, Paul. *New Reformation: Notes of a Neolithic Conservative.* New York: Random House, 1970.

Henry, Nelson B., ed. *Modern Philosophies and Education.* Fifty-fourth Yearbook of the National Society for the Study of Education. Chicago: University of Chicago Press, 1955.

Jourard, Sidney M. *Disclosing Man to Himself.* Princeton, N.J.: D. Van Nostrand Co., 1968.

Kneller, George F. *Introduction to the Philosophy of Education.* New York: John Wiley & Sons, 1964.

May, Rollo. *Love and Will.* New York: W. W. Norton & Co., 1969.

Mumford, Lewis. *The Myth of the Machine: The Pentagon of Power.* New York: Harcourt Brace Jovanovich, 1970.

Nakosteen, Mehdi. *The History and Philosophy of Education.* New York: Ronald Press Co., 1965.

Phenix, Philip H., ed. *Philosophies of Education.* New York: John Wiley & Sons, 1961.

Reich, Charles A. *The Greening of America.* New York: Random House, 1970.

Roszak, Theodore. *The Making of a Counter Culture*. Garden City, N.Y.: Doubleday & Co., 1969.

Schrag, Peter. "End of the Impossible Dream." *Saturday Review*, September 19, 1970, pp. 68–70, 92–96.

Suhor, Charles. "The Bogey Man . . . Search and Destroy." *Media and Methods*, September, 1970, pp. 78, 75.

CHAPTER 5

Brickman, William W., and Stanley Lehrer. *Automation, Education, and Human Values*. New York: School and Society Books, 1966.

Bruner, Jerome. *The Process of Education*. Cambridge: Harvard University Press, 1960; paperback Vintage Books, 1960.

"Collision Course in the High Schools." *Life*, May 16, 1969, pp. 24–25.

Colorado Advisory Committee on the Social Studies. *A Guide for Concept Development in the Social Studies*. Denver: Colorado Department of Education, 1967.

Dewey, John. *Democracy and Education*. New York: Macmillan Co., 1916; paperback Free Press, 1966.

Fraser, Dorothy McClure, ed. *Social Studies Curriculum Development: Prospects and Problems*. Thirty-ninth Yearbook of the National Council for the Social Studies. Washington, D.C.: Council, 1968.

Geiger, George R. *Philosophy and the Social Order*. Boston: Houghton Mifflin Co., 1947.

Henry, Nelson B., ed. *Modern Philosophies and Education*. Fifty-fourth Yearbook of the National Society for the Study of Education. Chicago: University of Chicago Press, 1955.

Hutchins, Robert Maynard. *The Higher Learning in America*. New Haven: Yale University Press, 1936.

Jourard, Sidney M. *Disclosing Man to Himself*. Princeton, N.J.: D. Van Nostrand Co., 1968.

Leeper, Robert R., ed. *Humanizing Education: The Person in the Process*. Washington, D.C.: Association for Supervision and Curriculum Development, 1967.

Lewenstein, Morris R. *Teaching Social Studies in Junior and Senior High Schools*. Chicago: Rand McNally and Co., 1963.

Martin, William Oliver. *Realism in Education*. New York: Harper & Row, 1969.

Mehlinger, Howard D. *The Study of Totalitarianism—An Inductive Approach: A Guide for Teachers*. Washington, D.C.: National Council for the Social Studies, 1965.

Miller, Richard I. "An Approach to Teaching about Communism in Public Secondary Schools," *Phi Delta Kappan*, February, 1962, p. 191.

———. *Teaching about Communism*. New York: McGraw-Hill Book Co., 1966.

Newton, Richard. "Concepts, Concepts, Concepts." *Social Education*, January, 1968, p. 41.

Petersen, Aage. *Quantum Physics and the Philosophical Tradition*. Cambridge: Massachusetts Institute of Technology, 1968.

Phenix, Philip H., ed. *Philosophies of Education*. New York: John Wiley & Sons, 1961.

Postman, Neil, and Charles Weingartner. *Teaching as a Subversive Activity*. New York: Delacorte Press, 1969.

"Revisions in the Secondary School Curriculum." *University of Colorado Studies Series in Education* No. 3: *Trends in Secondary Education*. Boulder: University of Colorado Press, May, 1969.

Walsh, W. H. *Philosophy of History: An Introduction*. New York: Harper & Row, 1960.

CHAPTER 6

Bigge, Morris L. *Learning Theories for Teachers*. New York: Harper & Row, 1964.

Bigge, Morris L., and Maurice P. Hunt. *Psychological Foundations of Education*. New York: Harper & Row, 1962.

Bloom, B. S., and D. R. Krathwohl. *Taxonomy of Educational Objectives: Handbook I, the Cognitive Domain*. New York: David McKay Co., 1956.

Calvin, Allen D., ed. *Programmed Instruction: Bold New Venture*. Bloomington: Indiana University Press, 1969.

Cox, C. Benjamin. "Behavior as Objective in Education." *Social Education*, May, 1971, pp. 435–449.

Fenton, Edwin. *The New Social Studies*. New York: Holt, Rinehart and Winston, 1967.

————. *Teaching the New Social Studies in Secondary Schools: An Inductive Approach*. New York: Holt, Rinehart and Winston, 1966.

Hoffmann, Banesh. *The Strange Story of the Quantum*, 2nd ed. New York: Dover Publications, 1959.

Krathwohl, D. R., B. S. Bloom, and B. B. Masia. *Taxonomy of Educational Objectives: Handbook II, the Affective Domain*. New York: David McKay Co., 1964.

Krech, David, Richard S. Crutchfield, and Norman Livson. *Elements of Psychology*, 2nd ed. New York: Alfred A. Knopf, 1969.

Mager, Robert F. *Preparing Instructional Objectives*. Palo Alto, Calif.: Fearon Publishers, 1962.

Maple, Frank. "Treatment by Objectives: Preliminary Draft of a Program Designed to Train Workers to Write and Adapt Treatment Objectives." Mimeographed. University of Michigan School of Social Work, October 10, 1969.

Maxwell, John, and Anthony Tovatt, eds. *On Writing Behavioral Objectives for English*. Champaign, Ill.: National Council of Teachers of English, 1970.

Montague, Earl J., and David P. Butts. "Behavioral Objectives." *The Science Teacher*, March, 1968, pp. 33–35.

Roszak, Theodore. *The Making of a Counter Culture*. Garden City, N.Y.: Doubleday & Co., 1969.

Smith, Frederick R., and C. Benjamin Cox. *New Strategies and Curriculum in Social Studies*. Chicago: Rand McNally and Co., 1969.

Teacher Corps Policy and Related Instructions for Proposal Development. Mimeographed. Washington, D.C.: Teacher Corps, 1970.

CHAPTER 7

Addington, Harold. "The 1.97–2.00 Syndrome." *Personnel and Guidance Journal,* September, 1969, pp. 6–7.

Battle, J. A., and Robert L. Shannon, eds. *The New Idea in Education.* New York: Harper & Row, 1968.

Beck, Joan. "Unlocking the Secrets of the Brain." Reprinted from the *Chicago Tribune Magazine,* September 13 and 27, 1964.

Bloom, Benjamin S. "Learning for Mastery." *UCLA Evaluation Comment,* May, 1968.

Carroll, John B. "A Model of School Learning." *Teachers College Record,* May, 1963, pp. 723–33.

Combs, Arthur W. "The Myth of Competition." *Childhood Education,* February, 1957, pp. 264–69.

Davidson, Henry A. "Competition, the Cradle of Anxiety." *Education,* November, 1955, pp. 162–66.

Davidson, Henry A., Merritt L. Schriver, and Herman J. Peters. "Should Johnny Compete or Cooperate?" *NEA Journal,* October, 1960, pp. 30–32.

Holt, John. *How Children Fail.* New York: Pitman Publishing Corp., 1964.

Liegerot, Giles F. "Is Academic Competition for You?" *National Association of Secondary-School Principals Bulletin,* November, 1961, pp. 148–52.

Melby, Ernest O. *The Deprived Child: His Gift to Education.* East Lansing, Mich.: Mott Institute for Community Improvement, Michigan State University, June, 1966.

Rosenthal, Robert, and Lenore Jacobson. *Pygmalion in the Classroom.* New York: Holt, Rinehart and Winston, 1968.

CHAPTER 8

Bloom, Benjamin S. "Learning for Mastery." *UCLA Evaluation Comment,* May, 1968, p. 4.

Bonhoeffer, Dietrich. *Letters and Papers from Prison,* rev. ed. New York: Macmillan Co., 1968.

Durant, Will. *The Story of Philosophy.* New York: Simon & Schuster, 1926; paperback Cardinal Giant, 1953.

Harris, Sidney J. "Authentic Teachers." *Chicago Daily News,* February 4, 1964.

Hooper, Bayard. "The Task Is to Learn What Learning Is For." *Life,* May 16, 1969, p. 39.

Riesman, David, Nathan Glazer, and Reuel Denney. *The Lonely Crowd.* New London, Conn.: Yale University Press, 1950.

CHAPTER 9

Roberts, Walter Orr. "Science, a Wellspring of Our Discontent." *American Scholar,* spring, 1967, p. 247.

Silberman, Charles E. *Crisis in the Classroom.* New York: Random House, 1970.

Wiener, Norbert. *The Human Use of Human Beings.* Boston: Houghton Mifflin Co., 1954.

APPENDIX A

Dewey, John. *Democracy and Education.* New York: Macmillan Co., 1916; paperback Free Press, 1966.

———. *Reconstruction in Philosophy.* New York: Henry Holt and Co., 1920; paperback Beacon Press, 1957.

Nisbet, Robert A. *Social Change and History: Aspects of the Western Theory of Development.* London: Oxford University Press, 1969.

Shermis, S. Samuel. *Philosophic Foundations of Education.* New York: American Book Co., 1967.

APPENDIX B

Allport, Gordon W. "Values and Our Youth." *Teachers College Record,* December, 1961, p. 218.

Foster, Richard L. "Educational Supervision: Dead or Alive." An ASCD address, Chicago, Ill., March, 1969.

Tobin, Richard L. "The Omnipotence of the Majority." *Saturday Review,* September 27, 1969, p. 18.

Tocqueville, Alexis de. *Democracy in America.* Translated by George Lawrence, edited by J. P. Mayer and Max Lerner. New York: Harper & Row, 1966.

INDEX